The
Garland Library
of
War and Peace

The
Garland Library
of
War and Peace

Under the General Editorship of
Blanche Wiesen Cook, *John Jay College, C.U.N.Y.*
Sandi E. Cooper, *Richmond College, C.U.N.Y.*
Charles Chatfield, *Wittenberg University*

Arms Limitation
Plans for Europe before 1914

comprising

On the Reduction of Continental Armies
A Proposal
by
Adolf Fischhof

A Propos du Désarmement
by
Augustin Hamon

The Limitation of Armaments
and
Limitation of Naval and Military Expenditure
by
**Paul Henri Benjamin Bastuat,
Baron d'Estournelles de Constant**

with a new introduction
for the Garland Edition by
Adolf Wild

Garland Publishing, Inc., New York & London
1972

Library of Congress Cataloging in Publication Data
Main entry under title:

Arms limitation plans for Europe before 1914.

   Reprint of 4 works published in 1875, 1898, 1906,
and 1912 respectively.
     I. Fischhof, Adolf, 1816-1893. On the reduction of
continental armies. 1972. II. Hamon, Augustin
Frédéric, 1862-   À propos du désarmement. 1972.
III. Estournelles de Constant, Paul Henri Benjamin,
baron d', 1852-1924. Reprot on the limitation of armaments. 1972. IV. Estournelles de Constant, Paul
Henri Benjamin, baron d', 1852-1924. Limitation of
naval and military expenditure. 1972. 1. Disarmament.
JX1974.A7694   327'.174   72-10896
ISBN 0-8240-0322-5

Printed in the United States of America

Introduction

In European history, the question of arms limitation (or disarmament) can be traced back at least to the seventeenth century when the beginnings of standing armies ended the custom of mustering troops out of service after the conclusion of campaigns or wars. The political history of most nations since that time is threaded with discussions connected to this issue. During the years when raison d'état *was invoked to defend military preparedness, the critical reflections of isolated thinkers on arms limitation made little headway. Not until the period following the Napoleonic wars, coincident with the formation of early peace societies, did the question begin to attract some official and popular concern.*

In the first part of the nineteenth century, the organized peace societies made their debuts, particularly in the Anglo-American world. Arbitration and disarmament were the means advocated for the creation of an international order that would obviate war. Yet even in the relatively liberal atmospheres of England and the United States where the young peace organizations labored, these ideas were largely regarded as "utopian." Liberal and reform groups gave little support to peace problems, preferring their

*concerns with domestic issues such as suffrage reform
and the abolition of slavery. In addition, many liberal
groups apparently accepted the necessity of large
armies and navies as requisite measures to defend
their societies from less developed ones. When
Napoleon III, for example, cautiously approached the
powers at the end of the Crimean War with a request
to consider disarmament, no serious response to his
timid initiative was evoked. In 1870-71, the
Franco-Prussian War further killed whatever feeble
official interest that might have existed.*

*The war elicited, of course, a new round of
tensions and increases in armaments, leading to the
famous arms race of the late nineteenth century, a
development that decisively impressed contemporary
consciousness. Liberal internationalists led the attack
on the escalation of armaments; one of the earliest
and most eminent voices raised belonged to Adolf
Fischhof.*

*Adolf Fischhof (1816-1893), an Austrian poli-
tician, enjoyed an impressive reputation at home and
abroad from his role as a major intellectual leader in
the revolution of 1848. After the suppression of 1849,
he was imprisoned and tried for high treason.
Although acquitted, Fischhof was denied his civil
rights until 1867 and was prohibited from any
political activity. Neither influence nor authority
accorded to "the wise man of Emmersdorf" could be
destroyed by these patently repressive methods, and
through his writings and contacts he continued to*

enjoy influence. His central concerns revolved around the nationalities problem of the Austrian Empire, the solution to which he proposed through federalizations well as the extension of cultural and language liberties for non-Germans in the Hapsburg state.

When he took up the question of arms limitation in his articles entitled "Zur Reduction der continentalen Heere" that first appeared in two parts in the Neue Freie Presse *(Vienna) on September 26 and 28, 1875, Fischhof caused something of a sensation. These issues represented a departure from his usual concerns. The two articles were then reprinted as a booklet and then were followed by a second book on the subject, where the publisher's introductory remarks observed that the proposals "had been fully appreciated in the newspapers of all civilized countries."*[1] *To demonstrate the impact of Fischhof's ideas at home, the publisher brought forth petitions from the municipal councils of Graz and Vienna (initially sent to the Reichsrath) which repeated many of Fischhof's ideas and which called for the convocation of a European congress of parliamentary delegates and an immediate reduction in the size of the army.*[2] *The* Neue Freie Presse *offered vigorous support to Fischhof, as did Garibaldi who wrote to him on December 12, 1875: "We shall follow you and if we are treated as Utopians today we shall not be blamed for sticking to the truth of which our children will reap the reward some day."*[3] *(Garibaldi's letter arrived too late for inclusion in the*

7

printed set of essays.)

Members of the Austrian Parliament, with the exception of the deputy, Johann Fux, were generally not interested. Fux eventually introduced a motion in favor of the reduction of armaments and for the convocation of an international meeting of the states to consider the subject. Although the Parliament never discussed the subject, it was also aired in a speech delivered by the visiting Spanish pacifist and member of parliament, Artur de Marcoatu (April, 1876). Marcoatu's speech was heard by 34 members of both houses who then passed a resolution favoring arbitration and an interparliamentary congress. But again international war intervened – the Bosnian War and the Congress of Berlin – and even this small group melted away. The interparliamentary meeting did not occur until 1888-1889 when the initiative of a French and an English group created the Inter-Parliamentary Union.

In this volume there is reprinted the English translation published by Humphrey William Freeland in 1875 which came out almost immediately after the original articles appeared in Vienna. The proposals mentioned in the introduction as well as in the appendix refer to Cobden, the well known spokesman for free trade. Striking similarities exist between Fischhof's ideas and Cobden's, as well as with Émile de Laveleye (1822-1892) author of "On the Causes of War" [4] *which can be found in the supplement to the Freeland edition. (Laveleye was president of the Belgian Peace Society.)*

The movement attacking expenditures of armaments argued that with mounting state demands for military expenses, no reasonable taxation policies could be developed, no solid investments could be made in social spheres, and much incentive for capital accumulation was destroyed. It was clearly a classically liberal approach. As a movement, it gained strength in the 1880s and in the 1890s and was well enough publicized to be a factor of considerable strength in molding public opinion. Merze Tate has observed that "during the decade 1888-1898, the question of disarmament claimed more attention from liberal writers and the press than at any previous time in history."[5]

In such a growing climate of opinion, socialist groups could hardly ignore the problem. Members of the organized, largely middle-class, peace movement which grew in Europe after 1889 often called out to socialists for cooperation. While ad hoc collaboration occurred occasionally, the organized socialist movement as well as the organized peace movement could hardly consent to a close alliance. In 1896, the socialist congress at London finally adopted the official stance that no international solidarity among states could be achieved without first eliminating the class distinctions which were at the base of all conflicts.[6] Most socialists adopted this attitude.

The journalist and sociologist, Augustin Hamon (1862-1945), however, developed a modified view of *the socialist position. As an independent socialist in the last years of the century, with a vague attraction for anarchism, he accepted the notion of progressing world solidarity through intellectual and economic communication, while rejecting the middle-class pacifist acceptance of* Vaterland *or* Patrie. *His booklet entitled* Patrie et Internationalisme[7] *contained a number of ideas bridging middle class and socialist internationalism, His essay, "A Propos du Désarmement" which is reprinted here, originally appeared in the journal he edited,* L'Humanité Nouvelle, *in October, 1898. This piece was not a general statement but rather a part of the lively discussion that had developed in European circles surrounding public announcement of Tsar Nicholas II's appeal for an official conference on the question of disarmament. (The Tsar's Manifesto, circulated by foreign minister, Count Muraviev, was the step initiating the convocation of the Peace Conference at The Hague in May, 1899.)*

According to Hamon, the Manifesto created "une immense émotion, un bruit énorme."[8] Enthusiasm, however, was mixed with skepticism and often, outright rejection. French reactions were understandably confused since the proposal for "disarmament" emanated from their ally. To some in France, "disarmament" meant making permanent the status quo *with regard to Alsace-Lorraine. French Socialists, who had little confidence in the Tsar and disliked the alliance anyway, were irritated by the*

10

INTRODUCTION

Russian initiative. Hamon was troubled by the possibility that Alsace and Lorraine would have to be renounced forever and even feared that if the Conference failed, war might break out. But overall, he hoped for a genuine agreement and reflected upon its possible consequences. Despite the idea that disarmament was unlikely under capitalism, the socialist position, Hamon speculated about the possibility of an agreement among the established powers. Here, he went beyond the usual expectations of peace activists who were mostly concerned with the development of a system of arbitration.

In this regard, they turned out to be more realistic than Hamon. The motion proposing a halt in the arms race for a five-year period, introduced in the name of the Russian delegation at The Hague, was not accepted by the other powers. Eventually the Conference merely declared itself in favor of the principle of arms limitation and requested that each national government study the issues. Léon Bourgeois, the leader of the French delegation, secured this face-saving device.

The author of the last two pieces reprinted here, Baron d'Estournelles de Constant was the second most important French delegate to the 1899 conference. A diplomat and grandnephew of Benjamin Constant, d'Estournelles de Constant was a center-left member of the Chamber of Deputies since 1895, but for the conference at The Hague, was given diplomatic status again. At the meeting he was more involved in the discussions about arbitration than about the limitation of arms. After the Conference, he was appointed a member of the Permanent Court of Arbitration and spent a great deal of time in a press campaign attempting to popularize the results of The Hague Conference. In numerous articles and speeches, he developed the idea that the arbitration tribunal should be seen as a first step towards a European federation. It should be noted that d'Estournelles occasionally connected the desirability of federation to the necessity of mutual defense against the "yellow peril."

He did not express much interest in disarmament until the creation of the Entente Cordiale. Before its completion, d'Estournelles had waged an active parliamentary campaign in its favor, arguing that this too was a major step toward European federation. At the end of 1903, he proposed a bilateral arrangement on naval armaments which brought down such enormous criticism, including attacks from Georges Clemenceau in Aurore, that d'Estournelles temporarily gave up the idea.[9]

In 1905 it appeared that the climate had improved, and so he reopened the question. In addition to general preparations for the second Hague Conference, public opinion and national parliaments had to be interested enough to insist that arms limitation be put on the agenda. Both the Interparliamentary Union and the Universal Peace Congress passed several resolutions pressing for the calling of the next

Hague congress and for a specific agenda item on armaments. In his maiden speech to the French Senate, d'Estournelles repeated his proposal of 1903. This speech was translated into English and German and met a lively world-wide response. One English M. P., John M. Robertson, wrote that he would back the idea in the event a Liberal government returned.[10]

At the end of the year, a Liberal government did come to power and the prime minister, Campbell-Bannerman, stated that he thought his main task was to achieve a limitation of armaments. D'Estournelles quoted him in a speech to the French Senate,[11] *but he was less successful than his British friends. All through the year preceding the second Hague Conference, d'Estournelles reiterated the British position, including the Commons resolution of May 9, 1906, requesting that arms limitation be an item for the coming conference.*[12] *D'Estournelles could not get the French government to agree publicly.*

Campbell-Bannerman invited the Interparliamentary Union to hold its 1906 meeting in London in the hopes that more publicity could be given to the question of arms limitation. Furthermore, the prime minister offered considerable public support to the meeting and welcomed it with a warm address. At the meeting, d'Estournelles delivered a long report on the question of the limitation of arms which is reprinted here. At the close of the congress, the delegates resolved to support the House of Commons resolution at home and to move for serious study of the arms question in their own national environments.

D'Estournelles' report, translated into French, German, and even Esperanto, was distributed widely. A party congress of the French Radicals endorsed it, but because of the delicacy of the subject and depth of opposition even to considering it at The Hague in 1907, it was never seriously entertained among officials. Prior to the opening of the second Hague Conference, Russian and English diplomats came to terms and devised an innocuous resolution. Less time was devoted to the issue in 1907 than in 1899. Sir Edward Fry, representing Great Britain, observed that the arms race was a major problem for all nations, that it presented mutual disadvantages and that the nations should be asked to study the problem. This position was adopted by acclamation; d'Estournelles, again a French delegate, was deeply disappointed.

Worse was what followed the Conference — a new and noticeable increase in competitive armaments with emphasis on navies. Some justified the new round by pointing to the failure of The Hague to settle the problem. Many who previously had supported d'Estournelles' arguments, now demanded vigorous defensive measures against heightened threats. D'Estournelles fought a losing battle in the Senate against more battle-cruisers, and at one point, he even argued in favor of aerial navigation as being a less expensive form of defense.

In recognition of his efforts against armaments, the

14

INTRODUCTION

Council of the Interparliamentary Union nominated d'Estournelles in 1910 to chair its committee studying the subject. Others included the Englishman, Lord Weardale, the German, Haussmann, and the Russian, Miliukov. The results of their consultations was a report which was eventually presented to the 1912 meeting in Geneva but was published in 1911 in English, French, and German and excerpted in such journals as the Revue de Droit International, Nord un Süd, *and* Österreichische Rundschau. *Although the 1912 meeting of the Union accepted the report and passed a resolution affirming the 1906 points, little of practical value emerged especially as the international atmosphere grew more poisoned each month. While the peace societies continued and heightened their activities, helped by a large allowance from the European center of the Carnegie Endowment (of which d'Estournelles was a director), they could not cope with the forces drifting to war.*

The bitterness and frustation of peace workers who struggled in the futile work of avoiding World War I was shared by d'Estournelles who said to the assembly of the Geneva meeting where he presented his second report on arms limitation:

> *I have tried to protest before the parliament of my country in vain; I have always struggled; I have frequently committed political "suicide" . . . , or better stated in the charming phrase of one of my colleagues, I have made myself ineffective.*[13]

But, d'Estournelles also explained why he had devoted himself to a cause so politically unprofitable:

War, gentlemen, is only imminent if we want it enough and if our weakness brings it on.[14]

While the war in 1914 can be seen as a product of the weakness of peace advocates, nonetheless these people had done the very most they could.

March, 1972
Dr. Adolf Wild
Mainz-Mombach

16

INTRODUCTION

NOTES

[1] *Adolf Fischhof,* Zur Reduction der continentalen Heere, *Zweites heft (Vienna, 1875), p. iv.*

[2] Ibid., *p. iv ff.*

[3] *Richard Charmatz,* Adolf Fischhof *(Stuttgart/Berlin, 1910), p. 412.*

[4] *This essay is also reprinted in the Garland Library of* War and Peace *series (1971).*

[5] *Merze Tate,* The Disarmament Illusion *(New York, 1942), p. 53.*

[6] Ibid., *p. 64.*

[7] *Published in Paris, 1896.*

[8] *"A propos du désarmement,"* L'Humanité Nouvelle, *p. 445.*

[9] *D'Estournelles de Constant, Paul Henri Benjamin Bastiat, Baron, "Les Deux Sourds,"* Le Matin, *December 2, 1905.*

[10] *John M. Robertson, "La Réduction des armements"* L'Européen *(Paris), no.. 77, April 22, 1905.*

[11] Journal Officiel *(Sénat), April 9, 1906.*

[12] *D'Estournelles de Constant,* La Limitation des armements. *Lettre à M. Thomson, Ministre de la Marine in* Le Temps, *May 13, 1906.*

[13] Annuaire de l'Union Interparlementaire, *3e année (Brussels, 1913), p. 45.*

[14] Ibid., *p. 44.*

ON

THE REDUCTION

OF

CONTINENTAL ARMIES.

A PROPOSAL BY

DR. ADOLPH FISCHHOF,

OF VIENNA.

TRANSLATED FROM THE GERMAN, WITH PREFACE AND APPENDIX, BY

HUMPHRY WILLIAM FREELAND,

M.A., F.R.A.S.; LATE M.P. FOR CHICHESTER;
CORRESPONDING MEMBER OF THE NEW YORK HISTORICAL SOCIETY.

WILLIAMS AND NORGATE,

14, HENRIETTA STREET, COVENT GARDEN, LONDON;
AND
20, SOUTH FREDERICK STREET, EDINBURGH.

WILLIAM RIDGWAY, 169, PICCADILLY.

1875.

LONDON:
PRINTED BY WILLIAM CLOWES AND SONS, STAMFORD STREET,
AND CHARING CROSS.

"Blessed are the Peacemakers: for they shall be called the children of God."

"If the salt hath lost its savour, wherewith shall it be salted?"

Sermon on the Mount, Matthew v. 9, 13.

———

Ἄρες, Ἄρες, βροτολοιγέ, μιαιφόνε, τειχεσιπλῆτα.

Homer's *Iliad,* v. 31.

Ἔχθιστος δέ μοί ἐσσι θεῶν οἳ Ὄλυμπον ἔχουσιν·
Αἰεὶ γάρ τοι ἔρις τε φίλη πόλεμοί τε, μάχαι τε.

Ibid. v. 890.

———

"I envy not the tyrant's prize,
Red laurels in Fame's temple stored,
Be this mine Epitaph : Here lies
Who taught men to forego the sword."

See Chancellor's *English Essay,* Oxford, 1873, by Andrew Goldie Wood.

———

"The ships that travel between this land and that are like the shuttle of the loom that is weaving a web of concord between the nations."—Gladstone, quoted by Emile de Laveleye in his *Essay on the Causes of War, and the means of reducing their number.*

———

"Peace is the want of all nations, and, thank God, war is at the present day too costly to be readily entered on. I am convinced that the day will come when the civilised world will wage no more wars."—Louis Philippe, quoted by Emile de Laveleye as above.

———

"War is but murder on an extensive scale; and murder, on whatever scale committed, cannot deserve the name of progress."—Lamartine.

———

COLUMBUS AND LESSEPS.

Give to Lesseps and give to Columbus his due,
One discover'd a world and the other join'd two.
Fame not water'd by blood, as on History's page,
Crowns the heroes of Peace in the new Golden Age.

H. W. F.

RICHARD COBDEN.

We mourn for one whom mind, not birth, made great,
Who serv'd Mankind, his Country, and the State;
Whose public did with private virtues blend,
Adorning Statesman, Husband, Father, Friend.
The many toil for selfish ends, but he
Made cheap the poor man's bread, set Commerce free;
And freely therefore flows the poor man's tear,
While Nations bend in sorrow o'er his bier.
His dreams were of an age when wars should cease
In Brotherhood and Universal Peace.
He loved not triumphs in whose train appear
The Orphan's anguish and the Widow's tear,
But peaceful triumphs which in Home or Field,
Workshop or Study, Love, Art, Labour yield,
And triumphs to the Sons of Science given
When planets new reveal a larger Heav'n,
Or when through wires and cables, finely wrought,
A Wheatstone flashes instantaneous thought.

Disinterested, manly, truthful, pure,
He fought the fight, and His reward is sure;
Calmly he sank and left a name behind
In the affections of a world enshrin'd.

                                H. W. FREELAND.

A portion of the foregoing lines was written, many years since, as a brief and
imperfect but heartfelt tribute to the memory of a departed friend. The lines
relative to War and Peace have been recently added, with reference to the very
serious matters of which Dr. Fischhof's pamphlet treats. That pamphlet no man,
not excepting even our most staunch living defender of freedom as opposed to the
would-be tyranny of Ultramontanism, of peace and arbitration as opposed to the
haphazard barbarism of war, would have read with greater interest than the man
whose "unadorned eloquence," to use the words of another of England's greatest
statesmen, made him, whether in Council, in Parliament, or on the Platform,
the great, perhaps the greatest European apostle of Free-Trade, Brotherhood, and
Peace.

PREFACE.

THE question to which the following Pamphlet refers is one of those grave questions which call for decisive action in every centre of European thought. It is a question which comes home directly and indirectly to the pocket of every tax-payer in Europe—directly, in the shape of increased and still increasing taxes for warlike purposes; indirectly, in the increased cost of the necessaries, the comforts, and the conveniences of life, which the withdrawal of millions of able-bodied men from the pursuits of reproductive industry must clearly and of necessity involve.

One would think, to see the mad and suicidal rivalry, the hot haste of warlike preparation in which Christian nations are engaging, that Christianity meant nothing more nor less than the worship of Siva the Destroyer, and that its holiest rites were those which consisted in offering up hundreds, nay thousands, of human sacrifices on the altars of the savage god.

To the so-called heathens these Christian nations are constantly sending forth their costly missions. These missions are rendered futile to a great extent—partly because they carry with them, not simple morality, and that Christianity of which a life of love is the essence, but the dogmas of an antiquated theology, at variance with reason and common sense; and partly because these heathens say, and say with justice: "At home, the Christianity of the nations which you represent seems chiefly to consist in making war, or in making preparations for it. The resources of your mental and material wealth are taxed to the very utmost in rendering more complete the deadly implements and appliances which you possess for the destruction of your fellow-men. Is this, indeed, your Christianity—a Christianity teaching by example?"

I can add but little to those dark and gloomy shadows in the picture of the present state of Europe which Dr. Fischhof's graphic pen has drawn.

Something must be done if Europe is to be rescued from the burthens of an ever-increasing taxation for warlike purposes, and from an ever-increasing risk of widespread conflagration which the heaping-up of masses of inflammable materials must of itself imply.

Three questions then arise :—

1. What is that something?
2. How is it to be done?
3. Who is to do it?

To the first of these three questions Dr. Fischhof's pamphlet, by its title and its contents, gives the following answer: A simultaneous and proportionate reduction of Continental armies. The question of Land Forces is, of course, the material question, so far as the Continent of Europe is concerned; but the arguments in Dr. Fischhof's pamphlet apply, so far as circumstances furnish an analogy, to expenditure on Naval Forces as well. An overgorged appetite for ironclads has already contributed very largely to bring on, in the case of one Invalid on the Continent, an access of fever and disease, and "the Sick Man" now lies *in extremis*. He does not even pay his creditors the compliment of calling them together or consulting them, but, resting on a curious pedestal of effrontery, of despotism, and of insolvency combined, he says virtually, "I cannot pay you, and you cannot make me pay." What, then, can be done? Perhaps a European Commission, named by the Great Powers, may have to sell the Sick Man's ironclads to get a dividend for his creditors. There would still remain Turkey, a powder magazine, ready to explode or to be blown up at any moment. What can be done with it? The Great Powers of Europe ought surely at once to agree on some policy, not of expedients, but bearing on the face of it the promise of a permanent European settlement. Whether, if the Turk must go, and there seems to be no chance of saving him, Constantinople, declared to be a Free Port, and placed under their joint protection, would or would not furnish the point of departure for such a settlement, it must rest with them and with the public opinion of Europe to determine.

The passion for ironclads has affected not Turkey only, but other Powers upon the Continent. Men do not wish, when writing in the interests of Peace, to say anything that may stir up angry passions. France and Germany, however, and especially the latter, appear to be getting themselves ready for another struggle, by sea as well as by land. Do they want, for any purposes of peaceful commercial development, for any purposes but those of war, vast fleets of ironclads, to be paid for out of the hard earnings of the working classes in either country? Education and increased power are rendering those working classes more competent to discuss and more powerful in dealing with those serious questions of increased taxation for warlike purposes. Will these questions prove, or will they not prove, under such circumstances, a source of danger to the Thrones and Governments of the Military Powers of Europe, increasing in proportion as taxation for warlike purposes becomes more oppressive and extreme? Prudence would seem to cry with trumpet-tongue, to those who govern Continental States— "If, as practical statesmen, you wish to prevent revolution, and to strike a deadly blow at Communism, reduce at once your taxation for warlike purposes. Try rather, assisted by the margin which wise economy and prudent forethought will give you, to abolish, or to reduce to the modest level of fiscal requirements, those duties which press most heavily on the necessaries of life, and therefore affect most seriously the working classes. Strive next, by serious efforts, to improve the sanitary conditions of the homes in which they live. Strive then, by larger grants for elementary education, to which, chiefly at all events, State grants should be confined, to enable them more fully to appreciate the value of the concessions which you have made. Let works of education be, in part at least, re-written, that the heroes of war may not, except when they have fought in defence of country, home, and beauty, be preferred invariably, as hitherto they have been, to the far more useful and bloodless heroes of peace. By these means you may cut the ground from under the feet of Communism, and convince without flattering the working classes that you are their friends, and that happiness depends less upon this or that form of Government, Monarchical, Federal, or Republican, than on wise and beneficent fiscal laws, rooting in justice, which do not tax the people's food for the purposes of warlike outlay, but only for the comparatively trifling requirements of that revenue which must support the State."

As to ironclads, England, it may be said, outstrips in her outlay every one of the Great Powers. Very well; but the land forces of England are, as compared with those of Continental Powers, almost ridiculously small, and much dispersed. They are not only inadequate for purposes of aggression, but barely sufficient even for the chances of successful defence. Superiority at sea is therefore, for every one of her inhabitants, the sole condition of a good night's rest, to say nothing of the national existence. She has, moreover, not only to measure the naval forces of each of the Great Powers of the Continent, but to forecast the possibility—for I hope it is nothing more—of a combination of navies against her. When, therefore, the Great Powers of the Continent have shown, by substantial reductions of armaments, that they mean in facts, not merely in words, Peace, it will be time enough for English Governments to set to work to recast their Naval Estimates.

Without attempting in any way to circumscribe the limits within which, in the interests of peace, concerted European action may ultimately be brought to bear on the reduction of armaments, let me here make a suggestion which I venture to think a practical one. The instrument for maintaining the police of the seas is a flying squadron. Why should not each of the leading naval Powers tell off one or two ships to cruise together, and maintain it conjointly? Personal intercourse and personal friendship arising from such joint action, and a knowledge of languages, would do more to promote international good-will than is dreamt of in the chilling reserve of those who live wrapt up in a heartless mantle of self-enamoured pride and ignorance. M. de Laveleye, in his pamphlet "On the Causes of War, and the means of reducing their number," alludes, among other measures, to instruction in foreign languages, and in whatever relates to the condition of foreign countries, as a means for fostering community of views and identity of interests among nations. The study of languages, and of the condition of different countries, would be largely promoted by such an arrangement as that which I have ventured to suggest. I see no reason why, in the movements of this squadron of police supervision and observation, any notions of maritime supremacy or national jealousy should arise, or why those taking part in it should not share in an equal degree the honours of an alternating command, as well as of a generous emulation in a cause not narrow or self-seeking, but beneficial to the world at large. In order to promote such a study of languages as that which M. de Laveleye thinks desirable—and its importance cannot be overestimated—some of the younger officers of each nation might be transferred during a cruise into the ships of some other nation, so that the respective languages might be more easily acquired, and feelings of international good-will increased and maintained. I find it difficult to conceive any practical objection to such an arrangement.

As regards the second question which arises on Dr. Fischhof's pamphlet, his suggestion as to the Extra-Parliamentary action of Representative Assemblies is excellent, as far as it may be found practicable. All Conferences, such as that which recently took place at the Hague, of the Association for the Reform and Codification of the Law of Nations, in which America and the States of Europe were represented by members of Parliament, jurists, and others, must influence public opinion in the direction of peace and good-will, and adversely, therefore, to that rivalry in armaments against which 'Dr. Fischhof so eloquently protests. Why should not the Association just referred to hold an early Conference at Vienna, where members of Parliament and the Press are already discussing Dr. Fischhof's proposition? The discussion of the plan, if its details are not approved of, may provoke suggestions for making it more complete; and, while the Press is working, the agencies of the School and Lecture-room, the Public Meeting and the Pulpit, should be set in motion in every country. Chambers of Commerce, too, might add, if it met with their sanction, enormous weight to the proposal, and might affirm it at an International Meeting.

As regards the remarks made by Dr. Fischhof respecting diplomatists, it must be borne in mind that these men are but the mouthpieces of their respective Governments, which claim the right of giving extracts from, of editing or of withholding, the despatches which they receive. The public, therefore, seldom know more than a part of the truths which have been told by outspoken diplomatists.

Let me here say that the influence in favour of peace which an able diplomatist may exercise, especially when he is well acquainted with the language, literature, and customs of the country to which he happens to be accredited, is well illustrated in the case of our minister at Peking, Mr. Wade, who by successful mediation has prevented the outbreak of a war between Japan and China, and since, by judicious and skilful diplomacy, between China and England. May he long live to enjoy the satisfaction of having interposed to prevent bloodshed, and to bear the honour which the Government has conferred on him, with the full assent of an approving country.

As regards the third question above referred to, there may be good reasons why Members of the Austro-Hungarian Representative Bodies should take the initiative as regards Dr. Fischhof's proposals; though it might be a question, perhaps, whether the privilege of taking part in the proceedings of a Conference should be confined to Members of Representative Assemblies only.

The readers of an article on Austrian Finance, which appeared in the 'Pall Mall Gazette' of the 1st November, will know what those words "good reasons" mean. In that article we are told that Baron von Pretis, the Finance Minister of the Cisleithan Half of the Austro-Hungarian Empire, had recently laid bare with an unsparing hand, in his Budget-statement before the Reichsrath, the desperate financial embarrassments into which Austria has fallen. With an aggregate deficit amounting, for Austro-Hungary, to £4,270,000, one cannot be surprised at learning, as the article tells us, that Herr von Schmerling, President of the Austrian Delegation, in his speech at the last sitting of that body, should have complained of the constantly growing burthen of the Military Budget, and should have urged upon Ministers the necessity for retrenchment, advising a proposal of general disarmament.

As regards the place of meeting for such a Conference as that suggested by Dr. Fischhof, Vienna, if thought sufficiently central, might well be fixed on. His reference, however, to the former Congress held in that city is not, I venture to think, a happy one. What were the arrangements of that Congress, and where are they now? I may say, as was said by the able writer of an article in the 'Edinburgh Review' in 1832: "It is not our purpose here to follow the dark labours of this celebrated Congress. It met in the name of restoration, and separated with the imputation, if not confession, of having made partition the basis of its arrangements. It parcelled out nations, and fractions of nations, with the same indifference with which drovers in a fair, or West Indians in a market, separate and select cattle or slaves."

Let us hope that any Congress which the labours of Dr. Fischhof, or of Austro-Hungarian statesmen, may cause hereafter to meet at Vienna, will redeem the errors of Europe's clouded past in the sunshine of a better, a more just and more peaceful future; that it will not only meet, but separate in the spirit of restoration, and, by promoting reductions of expenditure for warlike purposes, restore the Budgets of European nations to those modest dimensions, and to that state of equilibrium, which tax-payers have a good right to demand; that—last, not least—by encouraging Free Trade policies, it will cheapen the costs of living for the toiling masses of Europe, and subserve the highest interests of European Peace. Should it do these things, no true friend of progress and civilisation will grudge the Imperial City the honour now claimed for her by her veteran philanthropist, of calling together and receiving a Congress so beneficent within her walls.

REDUCTION OF CONTINENTAL ARMIES.

The feeling of security and repose takes root most firmly in the consciousness of power. This holds true of the individual person, and still more of the individual State, which can only secure the right which it possesses power to enforce. The maintenance of the power of defence becomes, consequently, the serious duty of the State, and an imposing development of power becomes one of the most essential guarantees of its stability. It is, however, an essential condition of such stability that this external development of power should take place not at the sacrifice, but rather on the basis of an internal development of strength. The events, however, which are taking place on the Continent of Europe remind us forcibly of the conduct of that combative youngster who, while preparing himself for a gymnastic contest, deprived himself for many weeks of a large part of his food, in order to apply the money saved in paying for accoutrements and lessons in gymnastics. On the day of trial, however, he was greatly surprised at finding that he was utterly destitute of those forces for the acquisition of which he had made *such wise preparations*.

The peace of our days is a peace which brings no blessings. When a war is ended men no longer say as formerly: *Cedant arma togæ*: "Let arms give place to the toga." Arms are only hidden under the toga. Feelings of anxiety do not, therefore, even in time of peace, pass from men's minds. The spirit of enterprise is crippled. Commerce moves forward with cautious and halting steps, as if it were treading on the brink of a precipice. Nowhere is there a feeling of comfort or of confidence. Placed between inflammable materials on the one hand, and tons of powder on the other, how is it possible for Europe to look with feelings of comfort or of confidence towards the future ?

Nor is it the masses of the people only who can scarcely banish their anxieties any longer. The countenances of the upper classes betray the fact that they too "are sicklied o'er with the pale cast" of care and thought. A nervous excitability prevails everywhere which cannot possibly be mistaken. Journeys indicating tendencies, meetings between exalted personages, and peaceful assurances follow quickly on each other. Do not these assurances of peace, which almost every six months are renewed, point either to an imminent conflagration, or, at all events, to an apprehension of it ? It cannot excite surprise that this apparatus of war should, in the end, cause uneasiness even to those who have piled it up on a scale so vast and gigantic. Each of them has been trying to cause anxiety to the other, and is now himself filled with anxiety. In the giddiness of preparation, and the bluster of organisation, Governments now hardly know who goes first, or who follows after ; what is cause, or what is effect ; who is the threatened, or who is the threatener.

The worst feature of this general calamity is, that the masses of the people in all directions are looking in vain for a Deliverer. Were absolute rule still dominant in the great States of the Continent, the people possibly might look to Constitutions for a cure. But, except in Russia, the Parliamentary Tribune has been thrown open in all countries. In all countries there are speeches and perorations on army estimates, and in all of them Assemblies protest, and end by voting whatever is required.

What, then, it may be asked, do the men, whom the public trust, want insight, or courage, or devotion to those interests which they are appointed to watch over ? Certainly not ! Those men vote as they must vote—they vote under the influence of conditions which it is not in their power to change. A minister of war, when his budget is under discussion, directs the attention of the House to the enormous changes that have taken place in the character and condition of the armies of all the continental States. He then adds, in his own name and in that of his colleagues, words somewhat to the following effect: " It would be in the highest degree unjust to make us responsible for an increase of military expenditure which is forced upon us. We have no power to check its course abroad, and, in the face of universal armaments, to neglect it at home were treason to ourselves. Honourable members know very well that those only who have weight in arms can hope to weigh with words at the council-board of nations. If you wish that our words should not die away as empty sounds upon the air— that our interests should not be despised—if you wish that the existence of our State should not depend on the magnanimity of our neighbours, you cannot hesitate as to the vote which you should give." In answer to such appeals as this, how can patriotic Chambers refuse supplies demanded by a minister? Parliaments do not govern the European situation, they are governed by it. It is under the pressure of a state of things which is, in fact, equivalent to coercion, that Army estimates and supplies are voted in continental Parliaments.

Whence, then, come these conditions of coercion ?—whence comes this helplessness of legislative bodies in the presence of the greatest scourge of les which our age has witnessed We need not eng long or laborious inquiry to discover their origin. lies clearly and openly in the isolation of Parliaments, which, acting as a bar to mutual contact, and even to any approximation, admits no common point of union, no extension of the sphere of operations, no increased energy of action, by means of mutuality and solidarity. The representative bodies of each country are confined to their own narrow Chambers. No one yet seems anywhere to have thought of great Hall of Deliberation, fitted for the united parliamentary representation of our Division of the world. How would matters stand if the representatives of each people from time to time left room for a general representation of nations, and if Governments, on occasions of high importance, were made acquainted with the voice of Europe?

All the great interests of the age have sought, and found, their international rallying point. The Learned have their migratory gatherings; the Church has its councils; Trade its international markets; while Art, Industry, and Agriculture have created for themselves Universal Exhibitions. Only the common interests of Europe, which stand in need of parliamentary representation, have as yet found no middle point of union in which they might be dealt with as a whole. It is only the Public Opinion of our division of the world which, even for those political and social questions with which the welfare of its whole family of peoples is closely connected, has found no central organ to give it influential expression. Now, if there be any one interest which touches closely the European community, it is assuredly that which is connected with the diminution of public burthens; and if there be one question which, more than any other, calls for a rapid and happy solution, through the medium of some central organ of public opinion, it is beyond all doubt the question of Armaments. To bestow on this question a care commensurate with its importance would be the task of a general Representative Diet of Nations: a migratory conference of members coming from all the legislative bodies of Europe, or, first and foremost, from the centres of the representative Assemblies of the Great Powers of the Continent; since on them, more than on others, a reduction of armaments appears to rest, as a duty immediate and imperative. An assembly of this character, even if it consisted only of members of Parliament meeting together, without any special delegation, would exercise no small political influence; but much greater importance would attach to it, if those who took part in it were selected as delegates by the popular representatives of each country in a meeting Extra-Parliamentary.

In this case the International Conference, although destitute of any official character, or any legislative competency, would yet win for itself an authority and importance which hardly any Assembly ever possessed. The prosperity of three hundred millions of men would be closely connected with their decisions. That which is almost entirely withdrawn from the sphere of operations of individual Parliaments would be completed easily and quickly, through the medium of their conjoint action. The Conference alone might, by its appeal to Governments, succeed in bringing about a reduction of armaments, which, carried out by all the States of the Continent at the same time, and in corresponding proportions as compared with their present Peace Establishments, would not in the least degree alter the proportion which the forces of one Power at present bear to those of another.

This proportion of forces results, not from the absolute, but from the relative strength of the continental armies : from the proportion in which, relatively to the corresponding availability of the other requisites of power, the army and armaments of one country stand to those of all other countries. We may place ever so high, or ever so low, the numbers of the continental armies, but the tongue in the scales of power remains unmoved, so long as this proportion undergoes no change. Whoever—with a hundred arms—wrestles with a Briareus, has no more chances of success than he who, having two arms only, fights with a two-armed man. Of what use then is this gigantic outlay on armies, which, being incurred equally by all the Powers, is equally useless to every one of them? What good comes of this insatiable desire of soldiers and arms—this over-straining of strength which can end only in exhaustion? Is it statesmanship to imitate the prudence of that soldier who, through fear of being killed in war, killed himself in time of peace?

Reason and humanity alike appeal to Governments to display, henceforth, the same rivalry in disarming which they have hitherto displayed in arming.

To a rivalry so laudable the Conference might give a powerful impulse by means of two resolutions. The first of these would mark the quota of the existing peace establishments by which, in the opinion of the Conference, the armies of the continental States, or the Great Powers respectively, should be reduced. By the second resolution the members of the Conference would bind themselves to give in their respective Parliaments, in the course of their next ensuing session, a notice of motion somewhat to the following effect: This House confidently expects that the Government will, with as little delay as possible, make known to all the continental Powers, or, in the first place, to all the Great Powers of the Continent, its readiness to reduce the Peace-Establishment of its forces, in accordance with the quota named by the Conference, if the other Powers will do the same simultaneously.

The day on which the Conference passed such resolutions would be one of those days which have proved most fruitful in consequences in the history of our time. It would lead to the termination of a state of things which has only usurped the name of peace—it would tend to free the Continent of Europe from continual preparations for war, more intolerable than war itself—for war only tears away a part of the body, while continual preparations cripple the whole.

No deputy, to whatever Parliament or Party he might belong, would refuse his support to a resolution which relieved the whole of his fellow-citizens from a heavy burthen. No State, were its propensities ever so warlike, would have reason to look with disfavour on a measure which conferred as great a benefit on himself as on his opponent.

If the Conference declared with emphasis that this useless overburthening of taxpayers, this grievous sin of States against themselves, should not any longer be allowed, their voice of warning would not be passed by as unheard or neglected, even if it reached the ear of power, without the addition of that force which it might acquire from the echoing voice of Parliaments. Even in its fragmentary state, the Public Opinion of Europe has been named the Sixth Great Power. It might become the Universal Power if it made its weight efficient through concentration in a single organ. The planks of that tribune, from which would speak the representatives of nations in the name of nations, might henceforth with truth be said to represent the world !

Perhaps many readers who consider these proposals may ask : "Why seek all this new parliamentary machinery ? To bring about a general disarmament must be the mission of diplomacy." Very well; but has diplomacy ever yet attempted a solution of the difficulty ? Has the diplomatic action of the

European Cabinets given even the slightest indication of a wish, on their part, to take in hand this serious question which so urgently demands their grave and immediate consideration?

In that sphere of society in which diplomatists move, and from which they derive their inspirations, men are commonly much more keenly alive to the requirements which States make for the maintenance of power, than to those made in the names of Economy and Retrenchment. They have a very much keener eye for those political dangers which threaten them from without, if their means of defence are insufficient, than for those economical and social dangers which, notwithstanding their vast military expenditure, gather stealthily around them from within. Any help from that quarter is hardly to be expected. Those interested must strike the blow for themselves. When the question is one of diminishing a burthen, the initiative more naturally rests with him who has to endure that burthen than with him by whom it has been imposed.

If, however, the Cabinets most unexpectedly determined to play the game of Prevention, the meeting of the Conference would still be a pressing necessity. The reduction of war estimates is not a remedy that proves effectual, if applied in infinitesimal homœopathic doses. From the depths of its sufferings, Europe calls open-mouthed for a strong dose of this particular medicine. The hand which applies it must neither halt nor hesitate. A council of medical assessors must therefore watch over it, in order that there may be no wavering, no half-measures, and no neglect.

The reduction of armaments, moreover, is not the only international affair which requires to be dealt with by international representatives. There are masses of economical and social interests which certainly affect all people alike. Political questions of every kind and description are waiting for their solution by means of general co-operation. What could be more suitable for the examination of these than a Parliamentary Conference, not consisting, like diplomatic conferences, of men belonging in a preponderating degree to one particular sphere of society, or representing one class of vocations, but of men representing social positions and vocations of the most varied character? Europe has its destructive International—let us oppose to it a constructive International, in order to put an end to those dangers with which an Utopian demagogy threatens society. Had the shears been applied but once in good earnest to the exaggerated military estimates of European Powers, legislation would have supplied abundantly the means of working for reformation on an extensive scale. Popular representatives might then have been allowed time for the alleviation of social difficulties, and for an earnest endeavour to prevent works of humanity from being postponed or cramped by works of a destructive character. Matters would then, in the minds of statesmen, occupy the foremost rank, which, to our shame, have been hitherto left in the background.

In June, 1870, a proposal made in the Corps Législatif of France, that the nation should grant a milliard for social improvements, was treated as a monstrous proposition—a demand worthy of a lunatic asylum. In June, 1871, the nation had thrown away five times a milliard. For what? Let History answer the question. That is one example—one only out of many.

It is certain that in most of the countries of Europe the doctrines of Political Economy must be reversed, and quickly reversed, if they are to escape the curse of succeeding generations. To facilitate by a decisive policy this revolution, within the domain of political economy, would be one of the great tasks which the popular representatives would have to take upon themselves whenever, unfettered by the restrictions of individual Parliaments, they met together for Cosmopolitan action. Their action, at first connected by slight ties with that of individual Parliaments, would in time be attached to the latter, as it were, by organic growth. One might not be thought too sanguine for hoping that the Conference might, one day, be united, by even closer ties, with popular representations; and that the general Diet of representatives might be converted into a delegation of the European legislative bodies. On this important delegation would devolve the task of giving their advice and counsel on all legislative questions affecting the European community; and, further, when united with the representatives of Governments, of forming an Areopagus for dealing with international disputes, in order to place a barrier in the way of war—more effectual, certainly, than any which diplomacy has hitherto set up.

Let us answer here, by anticipation, two objections to our scheme. The first, as might well be foreseen, is raised less against the Conference itself than against its being called together at an early day. "No time," it is argued, "could be less suited for a reduction of continental armies, and an agitation in favour of it, than the present. By means of the Prussian military organisation, Germany has won a military preponderance, the continuance of which preponderance would be a standing menace to the security of neighbouring States. The other Great Powers of the Continent have, therefore, found themselves compelled to reconstruct their armaments after the Prussian model. This reform must have ample time to proceed uninterruptedly, if it is to receive its full development, and to place the military forces of these States on that broad basis of sufficiency for defence, of which Germany is already in possession. Every Government must energetically resist any attempt, if made at the present time, to interrupt the organisation now in progress, or to effect any reduction in existing Establishments, unless they are prepared to defeat by anticipation the very objects of the reform."

In this process of argument all that is urged, on the subject of the new military organisation, is right enough. The error lies in the conclusion which it has been attempted to draw from it: namely, that any efforts made at the present time to procure the assembling of a European Conference would be premature. Is there any one who does not know that the distance is very great indeed between the point at which an idea is started, and the point at which it is carried out in practice? Even under the most favourable circumstances, the Conference could not meet before next year. During the continuance of its session it must content itself with preliminary consultations, discussions of a general character, and the appointment of an International Committee. This Committee would have to examine the question of defences, and to present its report and proposals to the succeeding Conference. The sending in of the report of the Committee, and the resolutions of the Conference, could not follow until a year later; another year would be absorbed by the resolutions to be eventually adopted by the individual Parliaments. Ample time, finally, must be allowed for negotiations between the Cabinets of Europe, and thus we should get nearer to that point at which a general diminution of Peace-Establishments might take place without danger to the actual balance of power subsisting between different States.

With reference to certain details of Army Estimates, it is possible that a favourable result might be more speedily arrived at. Above all things, it is important to apply a remedy, as quickly as possible, to that evil in our modern military system which is most threatening in a financial point of view—the continual remodelling of arms and warlike appliances. In some respects the arms of modern times are an even more grievous visitation for the people of different nations than the necessity of providing men to bear them. As regards the latter, when a state of peace is established, the grants for the year can be projected with very tolerable exactness, and a regular Budget can be presented. But the necessity and cost of an entire change in the description of arms supplied to armies preclude all foresight and baffle all calculation. Science and the inventive spirit of man are, with breathless haste, producing new creations. Every minister of war stands hourly in danger of having his preliminary structures, though based on the most solid foundation of figures, overthrown by the invention of guns of a new calibre or pattern; and no taxpayer is secure from one moment to another that his pocket will not be emptied by some newly-invented projectile bringing its new taxes with it.

Is, then, this military quest of novelty an advantage to any single State? It can hardly be rendered advantageous even when aided by some watchfulness on the part of Governments. If one army is led on in a particular direction, the others quickly follow after. The accession of power is therefore *nil*, while the loss of money is immense. The International Conference might check this grievous evil, by proposing to the Governments a convention which would leave the parties to it free to bring every kind of weapon then in existence to the highest degree of perfection which it had ever reached in any army. If once this reform were carried through, then, in accordance with the terms of the convention, no single Power, if party to it, would be allowed, in time of peace, to make those changes in the character of the arms supplied to its soldiers, which now weigh heavily on Army Estimates. If in future science and experience should call urgently for an improvement in the pattern or manufacture of weapons, such improvement must, after a meeting of all the parties concerned, in the manner prescribed, be carried out in equal periods, and with an equal regard for the purses and finances of the several States.

A Convention of this kind would render it possible for the Government of every State to satisfy, in like proportions, the requirements of economy and of military progress.

It may be foreseen that occasion for an objection of the second character would be furnished by the attitude of Russia, who would not be represented in the Conference, in presence of resolutions arrived at by that Assembly.

This powerful State, say the objectors, could not allow that any body of men should adopt a resolution affecting it, without its concurrence. It is, therefore, greatly to be feared, that in St. Petersburg the demand for a reduction of armaments would be rejected, and that the efforts of the Conference would thus be rendered of no avail.

The anxiety which is here expressed rests on no sufficient ground. It must not be assumed that Russia would impute, as matter of blame, to the Conference, a defect for which that Conference was not responsible. The non-existence of Russian popular representatives would, of course, be an all-sufficient excuse for their absence from the deliberations of the Conference. "Il faut exister pour assister:" one must exist to assist. Moreover, the resolutions of the Conference would in nowise assume the character of absolute decisions. They would amount to nothing more than promulgations of public opinion. The final decision would be left to the free-will of individual Governments, including, of course, the Government of Russia. The latter would, therefore, hardly feel that it had any real grounds for running counter to the views entertained by the Conference. It is much more likely that it would be glad of an opportunity to effect important economies in its army estimates, with a view to the extension of its network of iron bands; since the colossal State stands far less in need of the forced augmentation of its armies than of the speedy establishment of good means of communication between the different parts of the empire.

From the side of Russia, therefore, it would seem that no danger threatens the work of peace.

There still remains this question to be discussed: Who is to issue invitations to an International Congress, in case the project of a Conference should find support in parliamentary circles?

The most appropriate persons for taking the initiative would be, without doubt, the popular representatives of one of the Great Powers of the Continent. We must, however, leave out of the question, at this moment, the national representatives of Germany and France. On this side, and, even more, on the other side of the Rhine, feelings are still so highly excited as to lead one to fear that an invitation from the Power on one side would be followed by suspicion and refusal on the part of the Power on the other side. The initiative might therefore rest with the deputies of Austro-Hungary or Italy; and then the observation would be fully justified, that the former Power ought to have the preference. Italy is the youngest of the Great Powers; Austro-Hungary, on the other hand, is a veteran among Great Powers, and a mission of peace devolving on Austria would correspond with its character as a State. Besides, this the kingdom of the Danube is inhabited by Germans, Latins, and Sclavonians, who are by race allied to almost all the races of continental Europe. It might therefore make an appeal to relations in the name of relationship, and invite them to join in a work of fraternity. Our parliamentary representatives, too, must feel themselves not only called on, but compelled to take a lead in the work of Peace; compelled by the condition of the empire, one half of which only bears up with pain under the present weight of taxation, while the other half almost breaks down under it. An opportunity presents itself, such as, perhaps, may never again occur, for an act full of glory, and for action embracing within its sphere the interests of the whole of Europe. Is it conceivable that such an opportunity should pass away, like the baseless fabric of a vision, leaving no results behind?

The Delegations from Austria and Hungary have now assembled.* It is only during the continuance of their session that the members of the two divisions of the empire enjoy the opportunity of frequent personal intercourse. If the idea of a Conference should be so fortunate as to meet with a sympathetic reception, abundant opportunities would be afforded to the deputies on both sides for an interchange of opinions respecting it. If they agreed to the principle of the proposal, a committee might very soon be formed which might arrange the formalities of invitation as well as the time and the place of meeting. This committee would also examine the question whether for the first Conference an invitation should be sent to the deputies of all the European States, or whether it would be advisable to address it in the first instance only to the representatives of the great States of the Continent. The report and the proposals of this committee would at a later period have to be laid before the representatives of both divisions of the Empire for their final decision. It seems almost superfluous to observe that the invitation to the Conference must be given by representatives to representatives in their individual capacities, not by representative assemblies to representative assemblies as such, and that all the meetings, deliberations, and resolutions in this matter must be regarded as *Extra-Parliamentary.*

As regards the first place of meeting for this International Conference, there can be little doubt about it if the invitations to it proceed from Austro-Hungarian deputies. Once already, during the present century, Vienna has seen brought together in its centre a Peace Assembly of almost unexampled brilliancy —a congress of princes to which it gave its name. Not less

---

* September, 1875.

splendour would be conferred upon the old and venerable Imperial City if, after an interval of six decades, it were chosen to be the first among the Capitals of Europe which should welcome within its walls a representation of the various nations of the earth—without example in humanity's past records—an assembly of European Notables which, while fulfilling its holy mission of peace, would bring blessings on the city in which it met, as well as on the world at large.

APPENDIX.

I.

COBDEN THE FREE-TRADER AND PEACEMAKER.

Φίλος δ' ἦν ἀνθρώποισι·
Πάντας γὰρ φιλέεσκεν.

Homer's *Iliad*, vi. 14, 15.

The connection between "Free Trade, Peace and Good-Will among Nations,"—I quote the motto of the Cobden Club,—is well illustrated in the Life, Speeches, and Writings of Richard Cobden. This is clearly and briefly shown in an interesting Essay on the Political Opinions of Richard Cobden, published by the Cobden Club, and written by a man who knew Cobden well, my esteemed friend Sir Louis Mallet, C.B., who is one of that Club's most active members. In the interests of Free Trade and Peace I should like to see the Essay to which I have referred translated into French and German.

The following brief extracts may serve to illustrate its tone and character:—

"Free Trade, in the widest definition of the term, means only the division of labour by which the productive powers of the whole earth are brought into mutual co-operation."—Page 51.

"The principle of Foreign Policy under a system of monopoly is national independence—in other words, 'isolation'; under that of free exchange it is international interdependence."—Page 34.

"Free Trade, or as Cobden called it, the International Law of the Almighty, which means the interdependence of nations, must bring with it the surest guarantee of peace, and peace inevitably leads to freer and freer commercial intercourse."—Page 15.

"A policy of Free Trade rests on the principle that the interests of all nations lie in union and not in opposition; that co-operation and not competition, international interdependence and not national independence, are the highest end and object of civilisation, and that, therefore, peace, and not war, is the natural and normal condition of civilised communities in their relation to each other."—Page 29.

The following is mentioned as one of the objects (No. 4) in the programme which Cobden appears to have set before him :—

" The reduction of military and naval forces by international co-operation."—Page 33.

" Cobden approached this question of reduction by two different roads. He endeavoured to bring to bear upon it international action, by arrangements for a general limitation of armaments, in which, as regards France, there appeared, more than once, some possibility of success, and in which he was cordially supported by Bastiat in the years succeeding the repeal of the Corn-Laws. He also sought, by every means in his power, to urge it on his countrymen, by appeals to their good sense and self-respect."—Page 42.

The following is mentioned among the causes under its own control which render a country liable to war :—

" The necessity of maintaining, for the purpose of repressing liberty at home, large standing armies which a Government may be compelled to employ in foreign wars, either to gratify the military spirit engendered by the existence of a powerful service or to divert public attention from domestic reforms."—Page 43.

" So long as the political condition of Europe is such as to render necessary, or possible, the large armaments which are a reproach to our age and boasted civilisation, while 4,000,000 men, in the flower of their age, are taken from productive industry, and supported by the labour of the rest of the population, no real and permanent progress can be made in the emancipation of the people, and in the establishment of free institutions."—Page 56.

" That the principles of public morality which Cobden devoted his life to enforce, will ultimately prevail in the government of the world, we think that no one who believes in God or man can doubt.

" Whether it be in store for our country first to achieve, by adopting such principles, the last triumphs of civilisation, and to hold her place in the van of human progress, or whether to other races, and to other communities, will be confided this great mission, it is not for us to determine.

" But those who trust that this may yet be England's destiny, who, in spite of much which they deplore, delight to look upon her past with pride, and her future with hope, will ever revere the memory of Cobden, as of one whose life-long aim it was to lay the foundations of ·her empire in her moral greatness, in the supremacy of reason, and in the majesty of law, and will feel with us that the ' International Man '· was also, and still more, an Englishman."—Page 64.

II.

THE EFFECTS OF CONTINUED WAR UPON A NATION.

Chancel lor's ' English Essay,' Oxford, 1873, by Andrew Goldie Wood.)

" Continued war results in a reign of force, in which men recognise only one method of settling disputes—by the strong arm. To this temper, so universal in ancient times, many of those customs and institutions which have specially operated to retard progress are due—such are slavery and the debased position of women."—Page 17.

" If the employments of Peace are really nobler than those of War, the song which delineates them should be noble too, and we may yet hope that the zenith of English poetry is not counted with the troubled Past, but still awaiting the country in a pacific Future."—Page 24.

" The Crusades inculcated that vicious form of intellectual pride, the belief that we are the sole possessors of spiritual truth. With an infallible Church, indeed, no other theory is tenable. But it is a theory which almost inevitably leads to the persecution of dissentients, though, fortunately for the world, the hand of the persecutor has rarely been more than partially successful. There is a vitality about thought. Docked and stunted though it may be by the most deplorable of all tyrannies, it springs out anew, and, watered by the blood of its martyrs, gathers new strength and vigour."—Pages 30-31.

" The Roman poet could look forward to a time when Rome should complete her imperial mission by teaching to the world the lessons and the rule of Peace. The Divine aspirations of Hebrew prophecy point with a higher sanction to the same blissful end. And when we look back upon the Past, in which each succeeding age displays less of the craving after bloodshed than its predecessor,—when we look around us in the present, and see the love of Peace striking down its roots into the deepest strata of Society,—when we realise the material and moral devastation produced by war, and see education leading all men slowly and surely to the same hatred of violence, is it chimerical to hope, or illogical to expect, that the ideal Peace of our day may yield to the real tranquillity of days to come, and that the world may yet see that truly golden age when ' War shall be no more ?' "—Page 35.

III.

ULTRAMONTANISM.

The dangers likely to arise from Ultramontanism for France and for the peace of Europe are sketched as follows by Mr. Gladstone in a powerful article on Italy and her Church in the *Church Quarterly Review*, October 1873.

" France, with all her wonderful, and in many respects unrivalled gifts, has yet, after a ninety years' apprenticeship, to learn the first lessons of the alphabet of political freedom; and her relation to the candidates for her government was well illustrated by Montalembert as that of a railway train, with the steam up and all things ready, waiting for the driver of the engine, when he who can first step up becomes, and for the time remains, absolute master of the situation.

" That powerful setting of the current of human motive and inclination, which we ill term Fate, seems to determine France towards another deadly contest with Germany for the hegemony of the Continent. No doubt her words, and, what is more, her thoughts to-day are those of Peace; but her under-thought, so to speak, the embryo of her mind in the future, which waits for its development, and for an atmosphere to live in, is war : war for recovery, perhaps more than for supremacy. When the time of that terrible war shall arrive, the very instinct of nature will teach her to strengthen herself by association with all the elements congenial to her purpose. Now such an association can hardly arise in the normal shape of alliance between State and State. Under this head she may possibly reckon, according to general appearances, upon the sympathy of Spain. But a country which after having risen so high has sunk so low, and which resembles France at present only in its incapacity for self-government, can count for little. The true ally of France will be an ally without a name; it will be the Ultramontane minority which pervades the world; which triumphs in Belgium; which brags in England; which partly governs and partly plots in France; which disquiets, though without strength to alarm Germany and Austria; which is weaker perhaps in Italy than in any of those countries; but which is everywhere coherent, everywhere tenacious of its purpose, everywhere knows its mind, follows its leaders, and bides its time. This minority, which hates Germany and persecutes Italy, will by a fatal and inevitable attraction be the one fast ally of France, if ever France be again so far overmastered by her own internal foes, as to launch again upon a wild career of political ambition wearing the dishonourable and fictitious garb of religious fanaticism. Thus, then, there are two great forces which, when the occasion comes, will menace peace: the political resentment and self-recovering energy of France, which has Germany for the object of its hostility; and the venomous ambition of Curialism, determined to try another fall before it finally renounces its dream of temporal dominion, which drives at Italy. And these two may in ill-assorted wedlock, even while hating one another all the time, band themselves together, in pursuit of their entirely distinct objects, by a common and identical line of action." *

* Let us hope that the danger to the peace of Europe which Mr. Gladstone anticipates from a possible alliance between Governments and Ultramontanism may not be so great even in the case of France as he supposes, and that his words of warning may tend to make it less. French statesmen have the warnings of their country's past history to guide them—they know well what an alliance with Ultramontanism, and its pet project the restoration of the Pope's temporal power, mean. In an able letter, written in the autumn of 1847, Lamartine stated that after studying Italy for twenty years he considered the temporal sovereignty of the Pope in the centre of that Peninsula an organic and almost insurmountable obstacle to the active, firm, and independent union of its States under a single rule. He afterwards defined the Papacy at Rome, in its character of a temporal power, to be "the union in a single government of the faults of all other kinds of government, without any of their redeeming advantages."—H. W. F.

LA GUERRE.

Louis XIV. mourant disait à son petit-fils : "J'ai trop aimé la guerre, ne m'imitez pas en ceci."—*Le Temps*, Dec. 10, 1875.

IV.

ON THE CAUSES OF WAR, &c., &c., BY EMILE DE LAVELEYE.
(*Cobden Club Essays.*)

The following brief extracts from the thoughtful and practical Essay of a distinguished Free-Trader and friend of Peace in Belgium will, I am sure, be read with interest by all who may take the trouble to study the suggestive remarks of the veteran philanthropist in Austria. Besides the passages quoted, M. de Laveleye's pamphlet contains an interesting sketch of the rise and progress of Peace Societies and of their organs for many years past.

" No question in Europe is more rife with troubles of a serious and durable nature than this question of Nationalities. The fermentation will not calm down until it has reached its end; and Europe may probably have to go through two or three more frightful wars before this ethnological evolution can be accomplished."—Page 12.

" But it is between Teuton and Sclave that the greatest difficulties are likely to arise, and for two reasons. In the first place, the national sentiment is in both races exclusive and grasping ; and, secondly, geographical necessities make it very difficult to draw boundary lines in keeping with the ethnographic requirements.'—Page 12.

" All these difficulties might be settled without war, Switzerland being proof. Switzerland is inhabited by three races, who live together in happiness and content, and with no desire to join the great surrounding nations with which they have ties of blood."—Page 12.

" *Affinities of origin are not without importance, but the first things for a nation are liberty, prosperity, and independence.*"—Page 12.

" The intervention of France in Rome even under the Republican Government, and the occupation of the Papal city under Napoleon III., took place to obtain the support of the French clergy, which exercises great influence over the rural electors. If a monarchical restoration were to happen in France, it is far from unlikely that, in order to conciliate the good-will of the Catholic priests, the new government would take in hand the cause of the Pope ; and there is a consequent danger of disputes and complications between France and Italy. In England, in Ireland, in

Austria, and in Belgium, the Catholics, guided by their bishops, have called for an active intervention in favour of the Pontiff. *If bishops, therefore, had been able to lay down the law to their governments, we should have seen already a new religious crusade.* Let us suppose, again, that Ireland were separated from England, and free to obey her own instincts, an Irish war with Italy for the temporal power might be predicted, and with it a war in Ireland itself between Protestant Ulster and the Catholic provinces."—Page 6.

" A war promoted by religious feelings is not therefore impossible even in our days, although the general march of ideas becomes daily more and more opposed to intolerance and to armed propaganda."—Page 7.

" One cannot say too often or too loudly that ministers of religion have in no country been sufficiently penetrated by the spirit of the Christianity they preach."—Page 7.

" They have not known how to instil into the hearts of men a horror, which they have not felt in their own hearts, of bloodshed, battles, and conquests. When the armies of their countries have been victorious, they have ever been ready to chant loud Te Deums, and they have anathematised war only when its issue was against their own cause. If the Spirit of Peace has made any way in the world, it is much less owing to the influence of the pulpit than to the influence of economic ideas. Cobden has done much more than any preacher to diminish the causes of war."—Page 7.

" In order that representative government should preserve a nation from war, it is not sufficient that the parliament should be elective. It should also really represent the nation; and the nation itself should be sufficiently enlightened to perceive what is injurious to it: the Chamber should likewise be composed of men independent and reasonable enough to resist the influence of the executive. In no great Continental country are these conditions fulfilled. In Prussia, as in France, the government can always obtain a vote for war, either by appealing to a feeling of excited patriotism, or by placing the honour of the country in an apparent state of jeopardy."—Page 22.

" The chances of war will decrease as representative government becomes more perfect, and as it exercises a more decisive influence on the resolutions of the executive.

" The Constitutions of all free nations should reserve the right of declaring war and making peace exclusively to their Parliaments.

" This stipulation, it is true, can hardly prove entirely efficacious, for it is useless in a country which has attained its majority, and in a country still in its infancy it would generally prove ineffectual. But cases may occur in which this precaution may operate as a veto on war, and for that reason it should be adopted."*—Page 23.

* In connection with these suggestions of M. E. de Laveleye I may call attention to Article 709 of the ' Draft Outlines of an International Code' prepared

D

" The hour will arrive for the establishment of a federation of nations with a Supreme Court like that of the United States, the decisions of which will be carried out by authority; but it is not yet come. True civilisation, true Christian sentiment, do not as yet exert a sufficient general and undisputed sway over nations.

" The High Court of Nations ought to be composed of the diplomatic representatives of the concurring Powers, assisted in their labours by jurists versed in international law. To prevent the susceptibilities of any great State from being hurt, it should have its seat in the capital of some small neutral country, such as Belgium or Switzerland. It should be permanent, as regards its formation, although it would sit only in the event of there being a difference to be settled. The court would be established by virtue of the special treaty promulgating the code of international law. It is important that it should hold a lofty position, to attract the attention and respect of the world; so that the pressure of the public opinion of nations might be brought to bear upon any State that should seek to evade the obligation of submitting a difference to it. Had the public known that the twenty-third protocol of the Treaty of 1856 morally compelled France, in her quarrel with Prussia, to call in the good offices of the other Powers before resorting to arms, its voice would probably have forced the French Emperor to take that step, and the war might have been averted."—Pages 36–37.

---

and proposed for adoption by my friend Mr. David Dudley Field, a jurist of whom America and all civilised communities may well be proud. I am happy in possessing one of the copies of that Draft Code sent to Europe as presentation copies, and without committing myself to an approval of every one of its 1000 Articles, I may with truth say that every one of them deserves the earnest attention of every large-minded jurist and of all unprejudiced friends of humanity.

Art. 709. No nation uniting in this Code shall commence a war against any nation whatever, without making public within its own territory, and as far as possible within the territory of the nation to be attacked, a declaration of war, assigning the reasons thereof, at least sixty days before committing the first act of hostility.

LONDON: PRINTED BY WILLIAM CLOWES AND SONS, STAMFORD STREET AND CHARING CROSS.

WORKS BY THE TRANSLATOR.

POEMS, ORIGINAL AND TRANSLATED.

LECTURES AND MISCELLANIES.
AXEL AND VALBORG; A Tragedy from the Danish.

Sold by Reeves and Turner, 196, Strand; and Wilmshurst, Chichester.

THE FOUNTAIN OF YOUTH; from the Danish of Paludan Muller.

Macmillan, London. Sold also by Reeves and Turner, 196, Strand; Wilmshurst, Chichester.

A Propos du Désarmement

by

Augustin Hamon

Reprinted from L'Humanité Nouvelle *(October, 1898)*

A propos
du Désarmement

Le 24 août 1898, le comte Mouraview, ministre du Tsar, remettait à tous les représentants des puissances étrangères accrédités à Saint-Pétersbourg, la communication suivante :

Le maintien de la paix générale et une réduction possible des armements excessifs qui pèsent sur toutes les nations, se présentent dans la situation actuelle du monde entier, comme l'idéal auquel devraient tendre les efforts de tous les gouvernements.

Les vues humanitaires et magnanimes de Sa Majesté l'empereur, mon auguste Maître, y sont entièrement acquises, dans la conviction que ce but élevé répond aux intérêts les plus essentiels et aux vœux légitimes de toutes les puissances ; le gouvernement impérial croit que le moment présent serait très favorable à la recherche, dans la voie de la discussion internationale, des moyens les plus efficaces à assurer à tous les peuples les bienfaits d'une paix réelle et durable et à mettre avant tout un terme au développement progressif des armements actuels.

Au cours des vingt dernières années, les aspirations à un apaisement général se sont particulièrement affirmées dans la conscience des nations civilisées. La conservation de la paix a été posée comme le but de la politique internationale. C'est en son nom que les grands Etats ont conclu entre eux de puissantes alliances ; c'est pour mieux garantir la paix qu'ils ont développé, dans des proportions inconnues jusqu'ici, leurs forces militaires et continuent encore à les accroître sans reculer devant aucun sacrifice.

Tous ces efforts pourtant n'ont pu aboutir encore aux résultats bienfaisants de la pacification souhaitée. Les charges financières, suivant une marche ascendante, atteignent la prospérité publique dans sa source. Les forces intellectuelles et physiques des peuples, le travail et le capital, sont en majeure partie détournés de leur application naturelle et consumés improductivement. Des centaines de millions sont employés à acquérir des engins de destruction effroyables qui, considérés aujourd'hui comme le dernier mot de la science, sont destinés demain à perdre toute valeur à la suite de quelque nouvelle découverte dans ce domaine. La culture nationale, le progrès économique et la production des richesses se trouvent paralysés ou faussés dans leur développement ; aussi, à mesure qu'ils s'accroissent, les armements de chaque puissance répondent-ils de moins en moins au but que les gouvernements s'étaient proposés.

Les crises économiques, dues en grande partie au régime des armements à outrance et au danger continuel qui git dans cet amoncellement du matériel de guerre, transforment la paix armée de nos jours en un fardeau écrasant que les peuples ont de plus en plus de peine à porter. Il paraît évident dès lors que, si cette situation se prolongeait, elle conduirait fatalement à ce cataclysme même qu'on tient à écarter et dont les horreurs font frémir à l'avance toute pensée humaine. Mettre un terme à ces armements incessants et rechercher les moyens de prévenir des calamités qui menacent le monde entier, tel est le devoir suprême qui s'impose aujourd'hui à tous les Etats.

Pénétrée de ce sentiment, Sa Majesté a daigné m'ordonner de proposer à tous les gouvernements dont les représentants sont accrédités près la cour impériale la réunion d'une conférence qui aurait à s'occuper de ce grave problème.

Cette conférence serait, Dieu aidant, d'un heureux présage pour le siècle qui va s'ouvrir : elle rassemblerait dans un puissant faisceau les efforts de tous les Etats qui cherchent sincèrement à faire triompher la grande conception de la paix universelle sur les éléments de trouble et de discorde.

Elle cimenterait en même temps leurs accords par une consécration solidaire des principes d'équité et de droit sur lesquels reposent la sécurité des Etats et le bien-être des peuples.

Quelques jours après, le *Messager officiel* de l'Empire russe publiait cette note que, le 29 août, toute la presse du monde reproduisait.

..

Ce fut avec stupéfaction, voire même avec quelque peu d'effarement, que le public accueillit cette circulaire, commentée partout.

La plupart des gazettes s'accordèrent pour célébrer le Tsar et son projet qui « faisait la joie et l'espérance du monde », comme l'écrivaient sous une forme ou sur une autre la *Libre Parole*, l'*Eclair*, le *Radical*, le *Journal*, etc. La personne du Tsar fut glorifiée en terme dithyrambiques. Il fut sacré Nicolas le Grand.

En ce concert de louanges détonnèrent les feuilles anglaises, nord-américaines, japonaises qui se montrèrent très froides, et considérèrent la proposition russe comme une utopie, un pur rêve sans résultats pratiques possibles.

D'ailleurs ce fut là l'opinion qui se manifesta le plus généralement. Quasi tous les journaux émirent des craintes sur le résultat pacifique de la conférence projetée, si même elle se réunissait, ce qui n'était rien moins que certain au dire du *Times*. Partout, on doute. En France, ce sont le *Figaro*, la *Fronde*, l'*Eclair*, le *Soleil*, l'*Echo de Paris*, etc. En Grande-Bretagne, ce sont le *Daily Mail*, le *Daily Telegraph*, le *Daily Graphic*, le *Morning Post*, le *Leeds Mercury*, le *Scotsman*, etc. En Allemagne, en Autriche-Hongrie, en Suisse, la même opinion se fait jour. La *Post*, le *Berliner Tagblatt*, le *Fremdemblatt*, la *Neue Freie Presse*, la *Kolnischer Zeitung*, le *Neues Wiener Tagblatt*, le *Journal de Genève*, les *Basler Nachrichten*, etc., sont grands admirateurs de la note du Tsar que M. de Molinari déclare paraître rédigée par un disciple de Cobden. Elles admirent mais ne croient point au désarmement. En Italie, la presse entière, officieuse ou non, se réjouit. Elle est enchantée et adhère pleinement à la proposition de l'Empereur de Russie, ne doutant point du résultat pacifique de la Conférence. Ainsi s'expriment le *Secolo*, le *Messaggero*, l'*Osservatore Romano*, etc. ; l'*Italia* fait exception. elle doute quelque peu. Le Pape approuve et joint la puissance de sa parole à celle du Tsar. En Espagne, c'est avec faveur que les journaux accueillent la proposition russe, espérant, comme on le lit dans *El Imparcial*, *El Heraldo*, qu'il en ressortira quelque bien pour leur patrie dans les tristes conjonctures où elle se trouve par suite de sa défaite dans la guerre hispano-américaine. Toutefois *El Globo* n'a aucune confiance et croit au maintien du *statu quo*, c'est-à-dire de la paix armée. En Suède, on est pleinement favorable. En Danemark, les résultats paraissent peu certains ; opinion que l'on trouve en Belgique où, cependant, le projet de Nicolas II est fort admiré par le *Journal de Bruxelles*, le *Patriote*, l'*Indépendance Belge*, la *Réforme*, etc. En Russie tous les journaux louent le projet et son auteur, leur Maître.

En France, l'enthousiasme de la première heure se calma vite. Les gazettes soulevèrent, avec plus ou moins de netteté, la question d'Alsace-Lorraine ouverte depuis 1871. Le *Petit Journal* et *L'Aurore*, sous la signature de M. Clémenceau, le *Gaulois* et l'*Eclair* sous la signature de M. Millerand, M. A. Naquet, M. de Marcère, etc., — la presque totalité de la presse française en un mot — observèrent qu'il fallait régler la question d'Alsace-Lorraine et la régler « conformément à l'équité et au droit imprescriptible des peuples ». Dans les feuilles, ce ne fut qu'épilogues sur « la consécration solidaire des principes d'équité et de droit sur lesquels reposent la sécurité des Etats » — termes même de la note — aboutissant toujours à la nécessité, pour la Conférence, de rendre l'Alsace-Lorraine à la France. Elles ne le disaient point nettement ; elles le laissaient entendre, mais déclaraient franchement que la France n'acceptait pas le fait accompli en 1871.

Outre-Rhin, l'opinion des journalistes était tout aussi catégorique, mais en sens contraire. La base de la Conférence prochaine ne peut être que le maintien du *statu quo* territorial. Voilà ce qu'affirment toutes les gazettes allemandes. Ce *statu quo*, c'est l'Alsace-Lorraine restant territoire de l'Empire d'Allemagne.

Donc, au seuil même de la Conférence, la question d'Alsace-Lorraine se dresse menaçante. Pour décider le désarmement, il semble bien inévitable de la résoudre préalablement. C'est là une terrible pierre d'achoppement. Aussi, est-ce justement, que, dans cette assemblée diplomatique réunie pour décider de la paix, MM. Clémenceau, Drumont, Naquet, etc., ont vu des menaces de guerre.

.*.

Ainsi que le constate la circulaire de Nicolas II, l'Europe entière est dans un état de paix armée qui la ruine. Un coup d'œil jeté sur le tableau statistique ci-joint et sur les graphiques I et II, fait voir quelle forte proportion des recettes budgétaires est absorbée par les dépenses pour la guerre. C'est en tous les pays une lente succion de tous les produits de l'énergie humaine appliquée à une seule fin : la préparation à la guerre. Depuis 1870, au dire de l'*Economiste Européen*, la politique de paix armée a coûté 45 milliards de francs !

C'est en France, comme le montre le graphique II, que les dépenses pour l'entretien des armées sont proportionnellement les plus fortes. Cependant, c'est la France qui paraît souffrir le moins de cet état de choses, j'entends au point de vue économique. Il semble que ses richesses lui permettraient de continuer longtemps le maintien d'une paix armée si coûteuse.

Les dépenses militaires auxquelles s'est livré l'Italie ont créé une situation budgétaire déplorable (1), encore qu'elle les ait réduites. Son intérêt direct

(1) Cf. Les Emeutes de la faim, par Nino Samaja, L'*Humanité Nouvelle*. T. II, p. 211,273 ; 1898, vol. 3.

TABLEAU COMPARATIF DES populations, des armées et des budgets généraux, de la Guerre, de la Marine.

Pays	Population	Superficie en kilomètres carrés	Budgets totaux en francs [1]	Budget de la Guerre	Budget de la Marine	Budget de la Guerre et de la Marine. Valeur p. 0/0 du Budget total.	Dépenses pour la guerre, sans la Marine, par habitant en francs	Armées de terre Officiers	Armées de terre Ss-Officiers et Hommes
France............	38.342.948	518.830	3.385.367.481	622.551.397	258.167.273	26.0	16.25	29.000	573.720
Allemagne........	52.250.894	540.521	1.508.117.830	676.881.478	107.800.307	50.09	13.00	62.087	557.283
Autriche-Hongrie..	41.394.956	625.337	3.245.491.193	111.619.257	35.203.150	11.7	10.60	25.176	331.717
Belgique..........	6.410.788	29.457	357.174.361	52.545.871	—	11.3	8.20	3.421	47.849
Bulgarie..........	3.154.375	99.872	90.957.609	22.171.671	—	24.7	7.10	2.600	37.000
Danemark.........	2.172.380	38.270	93.712.191	11.656.874	9.524.069	26.8	6.70	751	10.006
Espagne..........	17.365.632	507.015	757.765.658	110.225.391	23.433.911	21.4	8.10	9.315	70.829
États-Unis d'Amérique.	62.981.000	9.212.300	2.210.462.425	211.653.235	178.505.610	18.8	3.90	2.131	25.706
Grande-Bretagne...	37.879.285	311.628	2.111.108.925	461.500.000	493.140.000	39.0	12.15	10.143	219.199
Grèce.............	2.187.098	64.688	90.923.510	15.390.584	5.610.477	23.1	7.30	1.880	23.453
Italie............	31.102.833	286.588	1.712.571.166	269.175.843	99.336.646	21.5	8.60	11.238	920.460
Japon............	41.000.000	417.000	760.916.430	177.871.160	184.940.780	47.6	4.00	—	281.771
Pays-Bas.........	4.775.646	32.811	285.111.968	49.816.303	33.103.971	29.0	10.45	1.882	26.672
Portugal..........	5.049.729	94.819	247.150.315	26.104.380	18.635.390	18.1	5.10	—	25.658
Roumanie.........	5.376.000	127.181	209.928.010	42.499.160	—	20.2	7.65	3.080	44.000
Russie............	100.187.419	5.427.590	5.139.485.448	1.137.519.976	239.608.700	26.6	11.35	25.279	1.284.578
Serbie............	2.314.153	48.555	63.365.607	41.115.393	—	22.2	6.10	970	21.200
Suède et Norwège.	4.919.000	442.812	155.300.000	36.123.209	9.794.857	29.5	7.35	—	38.808
Suisse............	2.917.754	41.346	76.402.631[2]	23.012.361	—	30.1	7.80	—	—
Turquie[4]........	4.600.000	166.000	—	—	—	—	—	—	180.000
Total..........			22.734.352.474	4.453.622.534	1.696.254.900			151.953	4.026.203

(1) Il s'agit, ou de l'exercice 1896, ou de l'exercice 1896-97, ou de l'exercice 1897.
(2) Il ne s'agit là que du budget de l'empire. Si l'on y ajoute les budgets des États qui le composent, on a un total de 4.832.416.400 francs. Les budgets de la Guerre et de la Marine représentent alors 16.2 0/0 du budget total. En 1898 le budget de la guerre s'élevait à 631.838.125 et celui de la marine à 113.945.109.
(3) Exercice 1895.
(4) Les possessions immédiates en Europe sont seules comprises dans la superficie et la population. Il n'y a pas de budget en Turquie.

et même urgent est que cet état de paix armée cesse, afin de pouvoir dimi-
nuer son effectif de paix et restreindre ses dépenses militaires. Elle est donc
nécessairement favorable au désarmement.

Graphique I ; Comparaison des budgets généraux
et budgets de la guerre et de la marine réunis
pour les principales puissances. (*Les petites colonnes
avec hachures représentent les budgets de la guerre
et de la marine. Pour l'Allemagne, le budget général est celui de l'Empire.*)

Graphique II ; Dépenses
pour la guerre par tête
d'habitant.

La Grande-Bretagne, très riche (1), supporte très allégrement les énormes
dépenses qu'elle fait pour sa flotte. D'ailleurs, à cause de ses colonies éparses
sur la terre entière et de son commerce répandu en tous les pays, elle est
obligée de maintenir sa flotte sur un tel pied. Le désarmement, s'il concer-

(1) Cf. La situation économique de l'Europe, par A. Chirac, L'*Humanité Nouvelle*,
T. I, p. 605 ; 1898, vol. 2.

naît l'armée de mer, lui serait désavantageux ainsi que la presse anglaise le constata fort bien. Si le désarmement ne regarde que l'armée de terre, la Grande-Bretagne y est indifférente. Même, cela lui est plutôt favorable car elle peut espérer que cette diminution des armées affaiblira la Russie vis-à-vis de la Chine. Il est vrai que, d'autre part, elle peut craindre que des nations comme la France et l'Allemagne, débarrassées du souci de la guerre, ne consacrent leurs efforts à la colonisation, au commerce d'outre-mer.

L'Allemagne est en pleine voie de croissance industrielle et commerciale. Sans trop de souffrances, elle peut supporter l'état actuel de paix armée que, pour une part, elle a contribué à créer en exigeant, en 1871, la cession de l'Alsace-Lorraine. Riche, et en voie de le devenir encore plus, il lui est indifférent de faire des dépenses pour le maintien de ses forces militaires. Toutefois, très bien nantie, les mains pleines, son intérêt direct est à la paix désarmée de façon à faire progresser son industrie et son commerce. Elle ne désire point la guerre; elle ne veut plus de conquêtes; il lui suffit de garder ce qu'elle a. Un désarmement général, sur la base du *statu quo* territorial, la satisferait complètement et lui permettrait de disposer des sommes qu'elle consacre actuellement à son armée. Elle pourrait les affecter, soit à sa marine, soit à l'expansion de son commerce ou de son industrie. L'Allemagne, réserves faites du *statu quo* territorial, est donc favorable à la proposition du Tsar parce qu'elle sert ses intérêts.

La Russie est à l'aurore d'une période de développement industriel et commercial. Elle possède un immense territoire, une population considérable. Elle a besoin de toutes ses ressources pour les consacrer au développement de son industrie, de son commerce, de ses voies de transport. Elles sont énormes, ces ressources; mais une minime partie seulement est exploitée. Pour l'accroître, elle a besoin de la paix désarmée, d'argent. Moins elle dépensera pour ses armées, plus elle pourra disposer pour ses réseaux de voie ferrée. La Russie a donc intérêt au désarmement.

L'Autriche-Hongrie, encore que sa situation financière soit supérieure à celle de l'Italie, n'a pas des finances très florissantes. Elle préférerait par suite réduire ses dépenses militaires; d'autant qu'elle n'a aucune espérance de reprise territoriale, aucune possibilité de conquête. En effet, elle ne peut prétendre à reprendre la Vénétie; elle a acquiescé aux fruits de Sadowa. Vers le Sud, seulement elle pourrait s'accroître au détriment de l'Empire Ottoman. Mais cet accroissement est rendu difficile, voire même impossible, par la diversité des races peuplant déjà l'empire austro-hongrois, et encore par la diversité des races peuplant les provinces qui pourraient être incorporées. Le réveil des nationalités serbe, bulgare, monténégrine, macédonienne, grecque, rend très improbable l'augmentation de l'Empire. L'intérêt de l'Autriche-Hongrie est donc indéniablement de désarmer.

Les puissances danubiennes et balkaniques (Roumanie, Serbie, Bulgarie, Turquie), et la Grèce ont de si petites armées, des dépenses militaires si faibles que le désarmement ne les toucherait guère, tout en leur étant plutôt avantageux. La Suisse, la Belgique, la Hollande, le Portugal, la Suède et Norwège sont tout acquis au désarmement bien qu'il les atteigne peu, étant données leurs minimes dépenses réelles et relatives pour la guerre. Tout en n'acquiesçant point à la conquête du Sleswig, le Danemark subira le désarmement. L'Espagne, ayant perdu ses colonies dans la dernière guerre, n'a aucune possibilité de conquérir des territoires. Le désarmement ne peut que lui être avantageux en lui faisant restreindre ses dépenses militaires.

Les Etats-Unis de l'Amérique du Nord ne sont point atteints par le maintien du *statu quo* ou par le désarmement. Ils ne sont pas actuellement une puissance militaire. Leur extension industrielle et commerciale s'accomplit progressivement sans qu'ils aient besoin d'armée. Vis-à-vis de l'Europe, les Etats-Unis sont sensiblement dans les mêmes conditions que la Grande-Bretagne vis-à-vis des puissances continentales. Ils sont en compétition directe avec les nations européennes en Extrême-Orient. Si toutes désarment, le rapport des forces respectives ne changera pas. Et les Etats-Unis, qui ont une armée très faible, seront en bonne situation pour la lutte industrielle et commerciale. Par contre, la paix armée se continuant obligera les Etats-Unis à devenir une nation militaire, car ils sont entrés dans le concert européen par suite de leur victoire sur les Espagnols. Il leur faudra donc augmenter et leur armée de terre et leur armée de mer. Le désarmement général leur épargnerait ces dépenses et, à ce point de vue, il les avantagerait. D'autre part, les nations européennes disposant des ressources qu'elles consacrent à la guerre pour l'extension de leur commerce d'outre-mer, il en résulterait pour les Etats-Unis une intensité plus grande de la concurrence. En somme, l'intérêt des Etats-Unis est quasi indifférent vis-à-vis du désarmement.

Le Japon, civilisé à la mode européenne, a vaincu la Chine. Depuis cette époque, il faut tenir compte de son influence dans la politique universelle. En Extrême-Orient, le Japon se heurte à la Russie, à la Grande-Bretagne, aux Etats-Unis, à l'Allemagne, à la France. Plus l'armée de ces pays sera réduite, plus le Japon pourra lutter avantageusement en Chine pour la prééminence. Commercialement et industriellement, il lui sera plus facile de triompher sur le marché chinois. Il est donc plutôt porté au désarmement, mais il s'efforcera sans doute, avec les Etats-Unis et la Grande-Bretagne, de le restreindre aux armées de terre.

Les Etats du Sud-Amérique et de l'Amérique-Centrale n'ont pas encore adopté le système de la paix armée. L'Australie n'est point infestée par le militarisme. Ces puissances n'ont, dans le développement des affaires européennes, qu'une influence minime. Nous n'avons donc pas à nous en occuper.

Du rapide examen précédent, il résulte, pensons-nous : 1° la Russie et la Triplice (Allemagne, Autriche-Hongrie, Italie), ont plus ou moins intérêt au désarmement ; 2° la Grande-Bretagne, les Etats-Unis du Nord Amérique, le Japon y ont à peu près autant d'avantages que de désavantages s'il reste cantonné aux forces terrestres et y ont des inconvénients s'il s'étend aux forces maritimes ; 3° la France ne voulant pas acquiescer à la perte de l'Alsace-Lorraine, espérant ou paraissant espérer toujours la reprendre, n'a pas intérêt au désarmement.

.*.

Dans la Conférence, qui se réunira sans doute au commencement de 1899, la France réclamera le règlement préalable de la question d'Alsace-Lorraine. Elle élevera des objections au désarmement et elle sera seule à les élever. Elle apparaîtra comme le trouble-fête de l'Europe. Elle se trouvera par suite en une position fausse, isolée vis-à-vis de l'Europe continentale qui se dressera contre elle, vis-à-vis des puissances maritimes qui regarderont avec le secret espoir de profiter des circonstances quelles qu'elles soient.

Etant donnée cette situation si grave, comment se fait-il que le Tsar, allié de la France, ait lancé la circulaire pour le désarmement?

Aucuns ont pensé qu'il avait préalablement conféré de ce projet avec les puissances amies et ils entendaient désigner ainsi la France, voire l'Allemagne. D'autres émirent des doutes sur la consultation de la France, avant toute publicité. M. Clémenceau était de ceux-là, alors que M. Millerand ne doutait même pas que Nicolas II eût agi sans prévenir son alliée la République française. M. Naquet posait ce dilemme : Ou la France était au courant du projet et l'approuvait ou elle n'était pas prévenue. Dans le premier cas, elle abandonnait toute revendication de droit; elle reconnaissait la justice de la conquête de 1871. Alors, écrivait-il, la France est absolument domestiquée. L'Europe continentale marchait d'accord. La Conférence était faite contre la Grande-Bretagne. Dans le second cas, le Tsar était tout de même un étrange allié, agissant sans s'occuper des intérêts de ses co-associés. M. Drumont songeait à des dessous diplomatiques dans cet acte d'apparence si nette. Pour lui, Nicolas II n'avait été que l'agent inconscient ou conscient de Guillaume II. L'Allemagne s'était servi de la Russie pour faire présenter le projet de désarmement. Cela était d'autant plus plausible que : 1º au dire du *Daily Chronicle*, l'empereur d'Allemagne était dans l'intention de faire cette proposition lors de son séjour à Jérusalem ; 2º il y a quelques années, le bruit avait couru que Guillaume II allait prendre l'initiative du désarmement; 3º la presse allemande voyait en la Conférence une occasion de resserrer l'union du Tsar et de Guillaume II, afin que « des efforts loyaux pussent triompher en commun des oppositions à ce projet » — L'opposition de la France!

L'analyse de la situation mondiale fait ressortir combien le projet de désarmement est une menace pour la paix générale. Il semble avoir été lancé contre la France pour l'acculer ou à l'acquiescement de la conquête de l'Alsace-Lorraine ou à la guerre. Il paraîtra étrange que l'auteur de cette proposition si dangereuse — au moins en apparence — soit le Tsar, l'allié de la France. Un membre de la Triplice n'eût pas agi autrement.

Quoi qu'il en soit des causes qui ont fait agir le Tsar, on se trouve en présence d'un fait qu'il faut accepter : une Conférence va très probablement se réunir pour rechercher les moyens de maintenir la paix générale et de réduire les armements excessifs.

Quel sera le résultat de cette conférence? Quelle attitude y auront les diverses puissances? Quels sont les moyens pour réaliser le désarmement? Quels en seront les effets économiques et moraux? Ce sont là autant de questions qu'il est intéressant d'élucider autant que faire se peut.

.·.

Les délégués de la Russie, de l'Allemagne, de l'Autriche-Hongrie, de l'Italie et de toutes les petites puissances soutiendront, conformément à l'intérêt de leurs nations, la nécessité urgente d'une diminution des armées, d'une réduction des armements. Seuls les délégués français émettront des objections et, *conformément à l'intérêt de la France* (1), réclameront la solution préalable de la question d'Alsace-Lorraine.

(1) Lorsque nous parlons en ces lignes de l'intérêt des nations, nous entendons parler de l'intérêt des classes dirigeantes de ces nations. Dans chaque pays, la majorité de la population a un intérêt certain, immédiat à la paix. Paysan, ouvrier, petit commerçant, industriel — à peu d'exception près — médecin, avocat, fonctionnaires de tous ordres ont partout intérêt à la paix, car la guerre n'est pour eux que causes de souffrances, de ruines.

L'Alsace-Lorraine est-elle autant désirée par les Français que le disent les journaux? Nous ne le pensons point. Depuis 1871, vingt-sept ans se sont écoulés ; de nouvelles générations sont arrivées à l'âge d'homme. Elles ont à peine ou même n'ont pas connu ces provinces comme territoire français. Elles ne se soucient point de les voir retourner à la France. L'opinion générale parmi les hommes de moins de 40 ans, littérateurs, artistes, savants, ouvriers, paysans, commerçants, etc., — il

De ce sujet très brûlant, la guerre pourrait bien résulter. En effet, l'Allemagne se refusera à admettre d'autre solution que le maintien du *statu quo* territorial. Donc, la Conférence, avant même qu'elle ait à examiner le désarmement, se trouvera en présence de deux puissances absolument antagonistes, maintenant des droits contraires nettement caractérisés. Une rupture de la Conférence peut immédiatement en résulter et la guerre s'en suivre.

Dans cette guerre possible, la France serait seule contre toute l'Europe coalisée. En apparence, ce serait la France qui aurait les torts, ayant empêché d'aboutir la Conférence s'opposant au désarmement. La guerre serait très courte, et se terminerait par l'écrasement de la France. Il ne peut en être autrement puisqu'elle serait seule contre toute l'Europe coalisée... à moins — ce qui est toujours possible — que des inventions d'engins de guerre (par exemple l'aérostat dirigeable, torpilleur aérien), faites et exécutées pendant la guerre, ne permissent le rétablissement de ses affaires et la victoire.

D'aucuns, parmi les socialistes, croient qu'une guerre déchaînerait en Europe la révolution sociale. Il est peu probable qu'il en soit ainsi dans les conditions où aurait lieu cette guerre. La défaite de la France entraînerait sa disparition comme nation délibérante dans le concert européen. La prééminence appartiendrait sans conteste aux puissances autocratiques comme la Russie ou tendant à l'être comme l'Allemagne, car la Grande-Bretagne, en présence de la Russie et de l'Allemagne unies et victorieuses, serait en mauvaise posture. Ce serait en Europe, par conséquent, une réaction générale s'efforçant d'affaiblir, de détruire toutes les tendances des peuples vers leur émancipation économique (socialisme) et politique (anarchie). La défaite de la France serait un retard dans la marche du progrès humain, une calamité pour le monde entier.

Mais écartons cette hypothèse d'une rupture de la Conférence. Il est probable que l'antagonisme de la France et de l'Allemagne ne s'affirmera pas sous une forme brutale, sans espoir d'entente. Admettons donc que les autres puissances cherchent un terrain de conciliation, sauvegardant l'honneur et les intérêts des parties en cause.

Ce terrain, quel peut-il être? La neutralisation de l'Alsace-Lorraine, devenue territoire libre tout en restant de l'union douanière allemande. Cette solution agréerait certainement aux habitants de l'Alsace-Lorraine. Leurs charges budgétaires diminueraient. Restant dans l'union douanière avec l'Allemagne, les industriels et commerçants alsaciens-lorrains continueraient à avoir l'Allemagne entière comme marché; il n'en serait plus de même, étant donné le protectionnisme actuel, si l'Alsace-Lorraine, devenant indépendante, sortait de l'union douanière allemande. Ouvriers et paysans ne seraient ni mieux, ni plus mal. Donc cette solution agréerait aux Alsaciens-Lorrains. Il

faut avoir le courage de le dire et de le répéter — est que la guerre doit-être évitée, que la reconquête possible, probable même — si l'on veut — de l'Alsace-Lorraine, n'équivaut point les désastres d'une guerre. Ces hommes, en majorité, n'éprouvent aucun désir d'aller se faire tuer pour que Metz et Strasbourg soient villes françaises.

Si l'on invitait tous les Français à voter, *au scrutin secret*, pour le désarmement avec abandon définitif de l'Alsace-Lorraine ou pour la guerre avec la conquête *probable, même certaine*, je suis convaincu qu'une écrasante majorité serait acquise au désarmement. Si, au contraire, le *scrutin était public*, la majorité serait très faible, peut-être même se transformerait-elle en une minorité pour le désarmement. Dans le conditionnement des faits, un nouveau facteur serait intervenu : le respect humain. Par crainte d'avoir peur de la guerre, beaucoup voteraient contre le désarmement tant que l'Alsace-Lorraine ne serait pas rendue à la France.

nous semble difficile que les Français et leur gouvernement ne se rallient
point à une telle combinaison qui permettrait honorablement le désarmement.
En Allemagne, l'accueil de cette proposition serait sans doute moins favorable. Le parti militaire — et il est puissant — s'y opposerait avec énergie;
car ce serait l'abandon de la conquête faite il y a un quart de siècle, ce serait
la négation de ce qu'il avait soutenu : la nécessité pour la défense nationale
de l'annexion de l'Alsace-Lorraine. Guillaume II, s'il veut vraiment le désarmement sur terre pour disposer de ressources afin d'accroître la marine et de
concurrencier la Grande-Bretagne, serait évidemment favorable à cette
solution. Au contraire, la classe bourgeoise des industriels et des commerçants allemands fera quelque opposition, l'Alsace-Lorraine restant dans
l'union douanière. En effet, cela les constituerait en un état d'une légère
infériorité vis-à-vis du commerce et de l'industrie alsacien-lorrains, puisque
ceux-ci bénéficieraient de la nationalité allemande sans en avoir toutes les
charges. Quant aux ouvriers et aux paysans allemands, leur situation ne chan-
gerait point, quel que soit le sort fait à cette combinaison. Si, à la Conférence,
l'Allemagne s'élève contre la neutralisation de l'Alsace-Lorraine, elle le fera
sans grande énergie, pour ne pas paraître céder, mais son opposition ne sera
certes point sérieuse; elle ne sera surtout pas absolue.

Est-il une autre solution? La consultation des Alsaciens-Lorrains, par
referendum, pour savoir s'ils veulent rester allemands ou redevenir français.
Il se peut que cette solution soit proposée par une des petites puissances
assistant à la Conférence, voire par la France se souvenant de ce qui
s'est passé pour Nice et la Savoie. Nous ne pensons pas que les grandes
puissances autocratiques ou tendant à l'être (Russie, Allemagne, Autriche-
Hongrie acceptent une telle idée. Ce serait, en effet, reconnaître aux peuples
le droit de se posséder soi-même, de se gouverner soi-même. Nicolas II,
Guillaume II ne peuvent l'admettre. Ils ne le voudront pas davantage et ils
repousseront ce système.

Mais fût-il accepté, il y aurait encore des questions de détail très graves.
Les Alsaciens-Lorrains de naissance seraient-ils seuls votants? Les Allemands
immigrés, domiciliés sur le sol d'Alsace-Lorraine voteraient-ils ? Le vote
serait-il public ou secret? Selon la solution de ces questions, varierait le
résultat du referendum. Avec vote secret et vote de tous les domiciliés sur le
sol alsacien-lorrain, la majorité se prononcerait pour rester allemande. C'est
là l'intérêt de presque tous les industriels alsaciens-lorrains. Ils ont pour
marché l'Allemagne entière. En devenant françaises, leurs manufactures se
voient fermer en partie cet écoulement de leurs produits à cause du régime
protecteur. La conséquence serait une ruine plus ou moins grande des usi-
niers. En outre, beaucoup ont établi des usines sur le territoire français,
tout proche des frontières, ayant ainsi des manufactures des deux côtés de
la frontière, en France et en Alsace-Lorraine. Le retour de celle-ci à la France
inutiliserait une grande partie de ces usines doubles. La fermeture s'en
imposerait, d'où perturbation profonde parmi la population ouvrière soit
alsacienne-lorraine, soit française. Pour toutes ces raisons, nous pensons
que le referendum, avec vote secret, des habitants de l'Alsace-Lorraine abou-
tirait au maintien en Allemagne de cette province.

La Conférence devra, avant de discuter le désarmement, résoudre la question d'Alsace-Lorraine. Elle ne peut aboutir à la paix que dans ce cas-là seulement. Deux solutions s'offrent : la neutralisation de l'Alsace-Lorraine; sa
consultation par referendum. Il est probable que la Conférence choisira la
première solution.

Quoi qu'il en soit du système adopté, il en résultera, par une Conférence internationale, l'examen d'une conquête territoriale vingt-huit ans après qu'elle a eu lieu. C'est la négation pure et simple du droit de conquête affirmé par toutes les puissances. Pour que les puissances dans une conférence infirment ce droit de conquête, il faut que les conditions économiques exigent de toute nécessité ce désarmement. Après le règlement de la question d'Alsace-Lorraine, les Espagnols pourraient demander un semblable règlement pour Porto-Rico, Cuba, les Philippines. Le Danemark pourrait remettre en cause le Sleswig. La question d'Orient serait évidemment soulevée et sa solution — le droit de conquête étant infirmé — pourrait bien donner lieu à de longues et graves discussions aboutissant peut-être à une rupture, à une guerre européenne. Celle-ci, déterminée par d'autres causes que dans le cas où il en résulterait une de la question d'Alsace-Lorraine, aurait sans doute une autre fin. Les conditions en effet seraient autres et l'Europe se trouverait partagée en deux camps de force à peu près équivalente.

Mais en outre, si le droit de conquête n'existe pas — et la neutralisation de l'Alsace-Lorraine montrerait cette non existence —, le temps ne peut intervenir pour le créer. Alors on pourrait voir les Polonais revendiquer l'érection en Etat neutre des trois Pologne allemande, autrichienne, russe ; les Tchèques demander leur autonomie, etc., etc.

Cette révision des conquêtes par une conférence internationale ouvre donc logiquement la voie à toutes les revendications des nationalités conquises, fût-ce même il y a des siècles. Mais s'il y a des revendications, les puissances conférencières n'en tiendront nul compte, cela est certain. D'ailleurs, elles ne pourront agir ainsi que contrairement à la logique, en vertu du principe, que le plus fort est le maître d'agir comme bon lui semble.

∴

La Conférence a délibéré. Toutes les questions préalablement soulevées ont été ou écartées ou résolues à la satisfaction de tous. Supposons l'accord maintenu entre toutes les puissances qui vont aborder le fonds même des questions à résoudre d'après la note du Tsar, c'est-à-dire le désarmement et les voies et moyens pour l'exécuter.

La réduction des armées aura-t-elle lieu aussi bien dans l'armée de mer que dans l'armée de terre ? C'est surtout la Grande-Bretagne que cette réduction atteindrait, à cause de ses colonies éparses dans le monde entier, de son commerce s'exerçant partout. Elle opposera, à tout désarmement maritime un *non possumus* absolu. Les raisons ne lui manqueront point pour justifier cette opposition formelle. La flotte de guerre est le nécessaire soutien de la flotte commerciale, l'appui obligatoire des colonies. La Grande-Bretagne, dans la société actuelle, perd toute puissance si sa flotte est réduite, et à cela elle ne peut consentir. De plus, on peut, en cas de besoin, reconstituer une armée de terre en deux ans, trois ans, même en quelques mois. Une armée de mer exige 18 ans, 15 ans pour être créée à cause des navires, de construction si lente. A aucun prix la Grande-Bretagne ne voudra désarmer. Si les autres nations délibérantes exigent, d'un commun accord, ce désarmement maritime, ce sera la guerre de l'Europe contre la Grande-Bretagne. Elle ne sera sans doute point isolée et saura se ménager des alliances Si elle était cependant seule contre tous ce serait son écrasement certain — sauf toutefois la possibilité d'inventions de nouveaux engins de guerre. Il résulterait de cette défaite, une réaction générale dans toute l'Europe, une tendance à reculer, ou tout au moins un arrêt dans le développement de l'émancipation politique et économique des hommes. La Grande-Bretagne est, en effet, en Europe la puissance actuellement la plus évoluée au point de vue politique. Sa disparition, comme nation délibérante dans le concert européen, causerait un préjudice considérable au progrès humain.

Mais il semble improbable que cette éventualité se présente car l'intérêt de plusieurs des grandes nations qui assisteront à la Conférence est de posséder des flottes plus ou moins fortes. L'Allemagne désire vivement devenir une puissance maritime et coloniale ; elle veut accroître considérablement sa flotte. Elle appuiera donc la Grande-Bretagne dans l'intention de reporter sur la marine les crédits dont elle n'aurait plus besoin pour l'armée de terre. La France, soucieuse de ses nombreuses colonies, penchera plutôt pour le maintien de l'armement maritime.

Les Etats-Unis du Nord Amérique veulent devenir une puissance maritime et à leur tour essaimer en des colonies. Ils appuieront donc la Grande-Bretagne aidés en cela par le Japon. Il n'y aura guère que la Russie qui soutiendra la nécessité du désarmement maritime. En lutte avec le Royaume Uni de Grande-Bretagne et d'Irlande pour la prééminence en Chine, en toute l'Asie même, la Russie a besoin d'une Grande-Bretagne affaiblie, incapable de lui tenir tête en Extrême-Orient.

Les autres puissances délibérantes, à l'exception de deux ou trois, sont plutôt indifférentes à ce désarmement maritime, car ce qu'elle désirent par dessus tout c'est qu'une guerre ne vienne point troubler la quiétude de l'Europe. Et une guerre en Europe ne peut, sauf de rares exceptions, se faire que sur le continent, avec des armées de terre. Les flottes ne jouent en un conflit européen qu'un rôle très effacé. Peu importe donc que les nations restent armées sur mer. Il est probable que pour éviter une rupture et une guerre, la Conférence décidera que le désarmement n'atteint point les forces maritimes.

. .

Jusqu'ici nous supposons l'œuvre pacificatrice menée à bonne fin par la Conférence malgré les oppositions nombreuses, malgré les embûches dressées. En effet le désarmement va préjudicier foule d'intérêts de classes, de familles, d'individus. Tous se lèveront, unis pour résister à l'œuvre de paix. Toute la gent militaire professionnelle, en tous les pays, — et elle est nombreuse et elle est puissante en Allemagne, en Russie — manœuvrera pour s'opposer au désarmement qui l'inutiliserait, la déclasserait. L'état de paix diminuerait de beaucoup l'importance du personnel diplomatique dans le monde entier. Aussi diplomates et leurs familles useront de leur influence, de leurs relations pour résister au désarmement. Et cela leur sera d'autant plus facile, que ce seront des leurs qui feront partie de la Conférence. A ces efforts se joindront ceux de certains industriels, grands fabricants de canons, d'obus, d'explosifs tels que les Krupp, les Armstrong, les Schneider. Un désarmement général, en effet, bouleverserait leur industrie. Ils devraient la transformer sans être certains de retirer de cette transformation autant de bénéfice qu'ils en font maintenant. Les financiers, lanceurs d'emprunts d'Etat, comme les Rothschild, les Bleichroeder, etc., ont intérêt au maintien de la paix armée. Cet état oblige à des dépenses considérables et fait s'endetter les nations. Par suite, il sert directement les intérêts des grands capitalistes. La guerre à l'état latent, c'est-à-dire le *statu quo* actuel, c'est de nouveaux emprunts se succédant sans cesse ; c'est de nouveaux armements nécessaires remplaçant les anciens, inutiles avant d'avoir servi ; c'est une source ininterrompue de profits énormes, d'agiotages considérables. « La guerre est le temps de semence et de moissons des capitalistes », a dit

Paul Leroy-Beaulieu. Tous ces intérêts des militaires professionnels, des gros industriels, des diplomates, des grands financiers se solidariseront pour s'opposer à la réussite de la Conférence. Cette union d'intérêts communs se fera d'autant plus aisément que tous font partie de classes et de castes alliées entre elles par des liens de famille, des relations mondaines.

**

La Conférence rencontrera donc sur son chemin des difficultés de toute sorte : sourdes menées, opposition plus ou moins ouverte, mauvaise volonté de tous les dirigeants. Tout sera prétexte pour en provoquer la rupture.

Supposons cependant qu'elle a passé victorieusement le cap difficile des questions préalables (Alsace-Lorraine, question d'Orient) et du désarmement maritime. Tous les délégués sont d'accord : le principe du désarmement est hors de discussion ; il est convenu. Mais dans quelle proportion ce désarmement ?

Il n'est point question du désarmement complet, de la suppression de toutes les armées permanentes. Cela est impossible dans une société de forme capitaliste comme la société contemporaine. L'ordre capitaliste a au moins besoin d'un noyau d'armée autour duquel se grouperait la nation armée, au cas où les antagonismes nécessaires en la société capitaliste se résolveraient en des luttes violentes. La guerre économique par voie industrielle et commerciale appelle la guerre militaire. Les capitalistes ont aussi absolument besoin d'une armée policière, apte à maintenir l'ordre actuel et à imposer, par la force, la paix aux prolétaires peu satisfaits du sort qui leur est échu. Ce besoin d'une armée de police a été avoué maintes fois par les dirigeants eux-mêmes. Les faits l'ont trop souvent prouvé. Il ne s'agit donc pas du désarmement général, mais du désarmement partiel. Dans quelle mesure va-t-il s'exécuter ? Comment va-t-on y procéder ? Tiendra-t-on compte de la superficie, de la population des pays ; de la nature du sol et de la disposition des frontières ; de la valeur en courage, en vigueur et en science militaire des soldats de chaque pays ?

Il semble fort difficile, et même impossible, de tenir compte de la valeur des militaires professionnels, de la nature et de la disposition des frontières.

On sera donc amené à ne tenir compte que de la population et de la superficie des pays appelés à désarmer. Les graphiques III et IV donnent les rapports respectifs, pour les nations européennes, des populations et des superficies territoriales. Ce sera, sans doute, proportionnellement à la population — la superficie suit sensiblement le même rapport que la population — que s'effectuera le désarmement.

Mais dans le dénombrement de la population fera-t-on entrer la population des colonies? La Russie sera-t-elle estimée comme ayant 140.000.000 ou comme ayant 100.000.000 d'habitants ? Jugera-t-on que la Grande-Bretagne a 38.000.000 d'habitants ou 346.000.000 y compris les Hindous, les Australiens, les Néo-Zelandais, les Canadiens, etc.? Suivant la réponse, la proportion des troupes varierait considérablement. Ainsi, pour la France, si l'on tenait compte de la population coloniale, l'armée doublerait en nombre, alors que celle de l'Allemagne, ne serait accrue que d'une façon insensible. Il n'est pas douteux que les puissances coloniales ne fassent ressortir l'impossibilité, pour elles, de laisser leurs colonies désarmées. Au Congo, au Soudan, dans les Indes, etc., les Européens sont en contact avec des peuplades sauvages, des peuples barbares. Il leur faut nécessairement des troupes pour se protéger ! Par suite, la Conférence sera obligée, tout en admettant le principe de la proportionnalité des armées aux populations, de faire des exceptions, en autorisant les

Graphique III ; Superficies territoriales en kilomètres carrés.

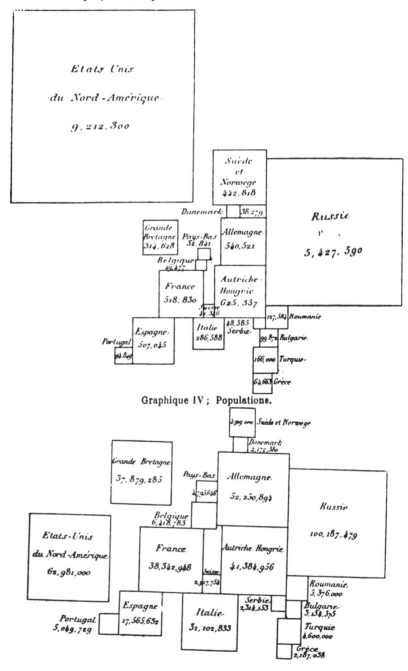

Graphique IV ; Populations.

pays à avoir des armées coloniales. Il est probable qu'elle décidera en même temps que ces armées devront rester toujours dans les colonies et ne pas dépasser, en nombre, une certaine quantité.

Supposons qu'il en soit ainsi. Tous les pays ont leurs armées réduites suivant une même proportion ; ils se trouvent par suite tous vis-à-vis les uns des autres dans le même rapport qu'aujourd'hui. La guerre serait donc tout aussi probable. Je dirai même qu'elle serait plus probable, car, alors, la guerre serait le heurt de quelques centaines de mille hommes tandis qu'actuellement ce serait le heurt de quelques millions d'hommes. Cette dernière quantité, par son énormité, par l'inconnu qui en résulte, étonne et, par suite, maintient la paix. La lutte de quelques centaines de mille hommes, c'est chose connue et chose facile. La guerre éclaterait donc plus aisément puisque la crainte de l'inconnu ne serait plus là pour arrêter les dirigeants. A côté des armées réduites, il faut, par conséquent, un tribunal d'arbitrage, une sorte de conseil amphyctionique aux décisions duquel toutes les nations devraient obéir. Ce serait ce conseil qui jugerait souverainement les différents entre pays. La création de ce tribunal d'arbitrage s'impose, autrement la mesure du désarmement partiel n'empêchera nullement la guerre ; elle la précipiterait au contraire. Naturellement, il faut, dans la société capitaliste actuelle, une sanction aux décisions de ce conseil amphyctionique. Cette sanction ne pourrait être que les forces militaires des nations confédérées obligeant, en cas de refus, à l'exécution des décisions prises. Aussi la conséquence de la création de ce tribunal d'arbitrage est la formation d'une confédération des Etats européens. C'est l'embryon des Etats-Unis d'Europe. Je ne sais si cela sourira fort aux rois et aux empereurs. J'en doute, à vrai dire. Aussi, il se pourrait bien que la création de ce conseil d'arbitrage fût très laborieuse. Pourtant elle est nécessaire, inévitable, car sans ce tribunal, le désarmement est un leurre, une duperie.

.·.

Et les armements ? Va-t-on les continuer comme dans l'état de paix armée ? Obus, canons, explosifs vont-ils toujours s'entasser dans les arsenaux en vue des conflits futurs ? Certainement non, car alors à quoi bon la diminution des armées. Dans quelle mesure les armements seront-ils réduits ? A combien de canons, à combien de fusils chaque nation aura-t-elle droit ? De quelque quantité d'approvisionnement par canon et fusil pourra-t-elle disposer ? A loisir, les délégués pourront discuter ; l'accord ne sera pas facile. Il le sera d'autant moins que toutes ces décisions sont à la discrétion d'une invention nouvelle. L'invention d'un engin perfectionné, par exemple du ballon vraiment dirigeable et pouvant servir de torpilleur aérien, inutilise tous les règlements de la Conférence. Une puissance, en effet, peut avoir de ces engins nouveaux sans contrevenir aux décisions prises, la Conférence ne pouvant prévoir toutes les inventions de l'esprit humain.

Qui surveillera l'exécution des arrêts de la Conférence ? La surveillance est relativement aisée pour la quantité d'hommes composant les armées; elle l'est beaucoup moins pour la quantité d'armes dont chaque pays pourra disposer.

Chaque pays a des forteresses, des forts, des camps retranchés ? Seront-ils détruits par ordre ou chaque nation sera-t-elle libre de les garder ou de les démanteler ? Chaque nation pourrait, en effet, continuer en secret ses armements et, à un moment donné, tenter une guerre de conquête, en Europe même. Il faudra donc, de toute nécessité, que la Conférence ordonne le démantèlement des forteresses, une surveillance pour l'exécution des conventions arrêtées.

L'armée, autorisée par l'accord international, comment sera-t-elle composée ? Faisons l'hypothèse que la France ait alors droit à 50.000 hommes, non compris l'armée coloniale. Comment se recrutent ces hommes ? Ils peuvent être tous des engagés pour un temps plus ou moins long ; c'est l'armée professionnelle. Tous les hommes valides peuvent être, soldats et appelés suivant un roulement tel que tout le contingent annuel (environ 300.000 hommes) passe dans l'année sous les drapeaux.

Il me parait difficile qu'un pays démocratique, comme la France, ait recours à l'armée professionnelle. Ce serait un regrès, un retour aux us d'antan, très préjudiciable aux intérêts de la démocratie. L'armée professionnelle ne tarderait pas à être, en effet, une armée de prétoriens, apte à un coup d'Etat et à toutes les mesures de coercition. Dans les pays où gouverne plus ou moins le parlementarisme et où le service personnel obligatoire est entré dans les mœurs, il sera difficile, sinon impossible, de revenir aux armées professionnelles. Seule en Europe, la Russie pourrait reprendre ce système, excellent pour renforcer son autocratie. En Grande-Bretagne, l'armée est composée de mercenaires et continuerait sans doute à l'être, sans qu'il en résulte des inconvénients pour la démocratie, à cause même du peu de considération dont jouissent les militaires en les Iles Britanniques.

L'armée coloniale sera, je pense, recrutée au moyen d'engagements volontaires, suscités par une haute solde. Mais sera-ce chaque nation ou la Conférence qui fixera le mode de recrutement ?

.·.

La Conférence est enfin arrivée heureusement au terme de ses travaux. Quelles seront alors les conséquences économiques et morales de cet état de désarmement !

Nous supposerons qu'après le désarmement, l'effectif des armées, y compris les armées coloniales sera le cinquième de l'effectif actuel. Les dépenses se trouveront par suite réduites dans les proportions des 4/5. Il résultera de là que chaque année, en Europe, 4.000.000.000 de francs environ qui servaient à la guerre pourront servir à la paix. Répartie sur les budgets de l'Instruction publique, des Travaux publics, des Postes et télégraphes, cette somme considérable aurait une action notable pour la propulsion du progrès humain. Il vaudrait mieux continuer à réclamer ces milliards aux contribuables que de réduire le budget, la réduction proportionnelle par tête serait en effet très minime, 15 fr. environ en France, 11 fr. en Allemagne (voir le tableau statistique et le graphique II).

La réduction de l'effectif des armées jettera dans la masse ouvrière et paysanne de l'Europe, plus de trois millions de travailleurs. Chaque année, environ un million et demi d'hommes, au lieu d'être appelés sous les drapeaux, continueront à rester dans leurs foyers. Pour vivre, tous devront travailler. Cette masse d'hommes agissant sur le marché du travail le déprimera. Les salaires baisseront ou tendront à baisser. Des conflits entre patrons et ouvriers surgiront fatalement plus ou moins graves. Ils seront plutôt plus graves, car, parallèlement à ce surcroît de travailleurs, il y aura une diminution de consommation. Soldats, tous ces hommes consommaient sans produire ; rendus au travail, ils consommeront moins car, si les besoins restent les mêmes ou sont accrus, les moyens de les satisfaire sont réduits. La production augmentera donc, puisque plus de producteurs, moins de consommation. Il y aura une surproduction momentanée et, comme résultat, peu après le chômage ; les conflits entre travailleurs et capitalistes croîtront en intensité sur tout le continent européen. La Grande-Bretagne sera à l'abri de ces luttes ouvrières, car la diminution de l'effectif des armées ne l'atteint que fort peu. Elle subirait seulement le contre-coup de ces perturbations continentales par suite de l'intensité plus grande de la concurrence sur les marchés asiatique et africain. A toutes ces causes de troubles viendra s'adjoindre la transformation des manufactures d'armes, devenue en partie inutiles, et la nécessité pour les ouvriers d'icelles de changer de travail.

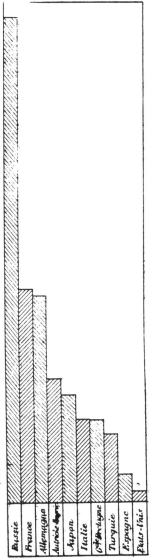

Graphique V ; État comparé des forces des armées sur le pied de paix.

Le monde paysan sera non moins perturbé. Le commerce et l'industrie des chevaux, ceux des fourrages seront modifiés, diminués quelque peu. Les travailleurs de la campagne seront bien plus nombreux ; les salaires subiront une dépression notable d'où émigration plus active vers les villes et aggravation dans celles-ci des conditions du marché du travail. Dans le milieu paysan, il résultera partout du désarmement un trouble local considérable, ainsi que dans le petit commerce. La suppression des nombreuses villes de garnison entraînera des changements profonds dans le commerce local de la boucherie, des produits alimentaires, des fourrages. Les cafés, les brasseries, les lupanars des petites villes ne subiront pas un moindre trouble, car ils n'auront plus ni soldats, ni sous-officiers, ni officiers pour les faire vivre. Il est probable que la consommation des alcools diminuera légèrement. Le paysan, en effet, ne va à l'auberge, au café que le dimanche ou les jours de marché ; le paysan devenu soldat y va toutes les fois qu'il a de l'argent.

Le désarmement aura encore une conséquence économique importante. Il inutilisera les quatre cinquièmes des militaires professionnels, c'est-à-dire environ cent vingt mille officiers de toutes armes (voir le Tableau statistique comparatif). Seront-ils purement et simplement renvoyés, à charge par eux de trouver les moyens de vivre s'ils ne les ont ? Seront-ils mis en demi-solde ? Auront-ils, leur vie durant, leur solde entière ? Les écoles spéciales militaires recevront, chaque année, un cinquième seulement du nombre des jeunes gens de la bourgeoisie ou de la noblesse, qu'elles reçoivent actuellement. Le reste devra donc rechercher une autre profession. Les uns se feront fonctionnaires. D'autres, ceux qui seraient entrés dans les armes spéciales, recoureront aux professions d'ingénieurs. D'autres deviendront des employés d'industrie, de commerce, très disciplinés, excellents dans les positions secon-

daires. Un petit nombre entrera dans les professions libérales. Les fils de
familles riches, qui, par snobisme, entraient dans l'armée, seront obligés de
rester civils et, comme tels, ils continueront à faire ce qu'ils faisaient étant
militaires, c'est-à-dire qu'ils continueront à manger leur fortune. Quoi qu'il
en soit, des proportions diverses dans lesquelles les professionnels militaires inutilisés envahiront les professions civiles, il n'en peut résulter qu'un
accroissement de l'acuité de la lutte pour la vie.

Tous ces troubles économiques, retentissant dans toutes les classes sociales
et particulièrement dans la classe prolétarienne, auront probablement une
très grande intensité. Selon certains, cette perturbation sera telle qu'elle
aboutira à la Révolution.

Les conséquences morales et sociales du désarmement seront non moins
importantes que les conséquences économiques. Le trouble sera profond
dans la noblesse et la très riche bourgeoisie. Volontiers militaires professionnels, les jeunes gens de ces castes devront, pour la plupart, y renoncer.
Comme l'entrée dans les écoles sera rendue plus difficile par le petit nombre
d'admissions, il sera nécessaire de travailler davantage pour y être reçu.
Aussi la jeunesse très riche abandonnera toute idée de revêtir l'uniforme
qui, par suite, tombera peu à peu en discrédit, les hautes classes ne le
recherchant plus. Alors, il arrivera ce qui est en Grande-Bretagne où le militaire ne revêt l'uniforme que pour les exercices et dans les cérémonies offi-
cielles. Il résultera de ces conditions que, chez la femme, l'amour de la livrée
militaire s'affaiblira insensiblement. Progressivement se formera un nouvel
état d'esprit dans la haute et moyenne bourgeoisie. Les exemples des
« hautes » classes sont imités par les classes « inférieures ». Ce même état
d'esprit se développera dans la petite bourgeoisie urbaine ou rurale, dans le
prolétariat des villes et des campagnes. On verra moins souvent des soldats,
puisqu'il y en aura moins, puisque les professionnels seront amenés à se
revêtir le moins possible de leur uniforme. Très probablement, ce nouvel
état d'esprit poussera à la modification du code militaire, cette survivance
des siècles passés, et même à la démilitarisation des soldats.

Cet état psychique nouveau sera beaucoup aidé dans sa formation par le
fait que personne ne sera plus déformé par un séjour de deux ou trois ans à
la caserne, sous la livrée de soldat. L'armée actuelle est, *dans tous les pays*,
pour ceux qui sont soldats occasionnels, une école de démoralisation, de
crime. Nous l'écrivîmes, il y a cinq ans, dans la *Psychologie du militaire
professionnel* et nous le répétons encore : le militarisme est l'école du crime.
La profession militaire détermine, chez ceux qui l'exercent, une déformation
mentale génitrice de crimes. La réduction considérable de ces professionnels
ne pourra qu'assainir, que moraliser l'humanité, en diminuant beaucoup le
nombre de ceux sur la mentalité desquels la profession agira. Après le désarmement, l'action de cette profession sera donc moindre et en quantité et en
qualité puisqu'il y aura moins de soldats et que les mœurs modifieront
l'exercice de la profession.

L'armée contemporaine est aussi école de discipline, d'obéissance. Insensiblement, tous les hommes, passant un, deux ou trois ans sous les drapeaux,
subissent cette influence de l'obéissance passive. Elle crée des individus
sans dignité, atrophie les individualités ou, par réaction, provoque parfois
une révolte désordonnée. Ces phénomènes, n'ayant plus de causes, cesseront
d'être. Si l'armée est toute entière professionnelle, ce sera un tout petit
nombre d'hommes qui seront déformés et alors le phénomène perd de son
importance. Si tous les hommes sont alternativement soldats, le court séjour
de quelques mois sous les drapeaux ne suffira pas pour habituer les hommes

à l'obéissance passive, à l'absence de dignité personnelle. Les quelques avantages qui résultent de la profession militaire — diffusion de l'instruction, fusion d'éléments ethniques disparates, homogénisation des individus — subsisteront avec ce système de tous les hommes passant successivement à la caserne quelques mois. Les individus changeraient de milieu et les horizons s'élargiraient. Les nombreux inconvénients du militarisme — expansion de l'alcoolisme, de la syphilis, de la paresse ; destruction de l'individualité ; accroissement de la servilité et de la prépotence, etc., — seraient supprimés.

En somme, le désarmement partiel de l'Europe la démilitariserait et diminuerait, chez tous les hommes, l'esprit d'obéissance, le respect de l'autorité. Il permettrait un plus libre développement des individus. Ce qu'il importe d'éviter, et cela est possible par une active propagande de tous les démocrates, c'est qu'il se forme, en chaque pays, une armée complètement professionnelle. Là est le danger et pour la paix future, et pour la marche de l'humanité vers un mieux être atteignant sans cesse un plus grand nombre d'individus. Il est à craindre que les populations, heureuses d'être débarrassées du service militaire, ne songent pas qu'elles se forgeraient des chaînes en acceptant la création d'armées réduites, purement professionnelles, d'armées policières. Il appartient aux socialistes de tous les pays, d'appeler l'attention publique sur cette grave éventualité. Comme des armées réduites professionnelles accroîtraient aussi les chances de guerre, il appartient aux sociétés pacifiques d'éveiller l'attention des peuples à ce sujet. Tous doivent provoquer par des brochures, des placards, des journaux, des conférences, une agitation qui enlève aux membres de la Conférence ou aux gouvernements toute velléité de créer une armée professionnelle, une armée de mercenaires, de prétoriens. Cette agitation aurait encore pour résultat d'inciter la Conférence à aboutir au désarmement. La pression de l'opinion publique aiderait à vaincre les oppositions sourdes ou franches que les intérêts lésés par le désarmement susciteront contre lui. Ce désarmement est, en effet, souhaitable, quelques importantes que soient les perturbations économiques qui en seront la conséquence inéluctable. Il sera un pas de plus dans la voie du progrès indéfini dans laquelle l'humanité marche lentement, trop lentement même.

.•.

Si la Conférence n'aboutit point, si les individus et les familles intéressés au *statu quo* triomphent grâce à leurs richesses, à leurs relations, à leur puissance de dirigeants, la circulaire du Tsar n'en aura pas moins eu une grande influence. Elle a provoqué une immense émotion, un bruit énorme.

On en a parlé partout, on en parle et on en parlera longtemps encore même si c'est à un échec qu'elle aboutit. Or, ce qu'on discute est envisagé comme de possible réalisation. Du temps seulement et cette réalisation survient. L'idée a insensiblement, inconsciemment même, pénétré dans tous les cerveaux. Et ainsi l'acte retentissant du Tsar aura plus révolutionné notre actuelle société capitaliste que maintes actions de révolutionnaires notoires.

A. HAMON.

INTER-PARLIAMENTARY UNION.

CONFERENCE IN LONDON,

23rd, 24th and 25th of July, 1906.

———◆———

Report

OF

M. D'ESTOURNELLES DE CONSTANT

ON

THE LIMITATION OF ARMAMENTS.

———◆———

LONDON :
THE PEACE SOCIETY, 47, NEW BROAD STREET, E.C.
—
1906.

LONDON :
PRINTED BY WERTHEIMER, LEA & CO.,
46 & 47, LONDON WALL, AND CLIFTON HOUSE,
WORSHIP STREET, LONDON, E.C.

LIMITATION OF ARMAMENTS.

———o⋅ₒ⋅ₒ⋅oₒ⋅ₒₒ———

MESSIEURS,

WE are assembled here in considerable numbers, members of most of the parliaments of the world, called together by a higher community of aspirations, notwithstanding the diversity of our institutions, of our languages, and of our customs. Together we represent millions of human beings enlightened by the same consciousness and animated by the same interest. We should, therefore, unite in seeking, in the spirit of patriotism and independence which has brought us together, for a remedy for our common difficulties. It depends on ourselves whether this voluntary mission shall be fruitful and that we shall not separate without result.

The question of the limitation of armaments is at the present time unquestionably one of the most pressing of all those which parliaments and governments are called upon to consider. It is put forward by the force of circumstances. As long as it remains unsolved it may be said that it bars the way to all kinds of reform and arrests the progress of civilisation. The Inter-Parliamentary Union has therefore been well inspired in undertaking the discussion of this question. By doing so it has responded to a universal desire. It will be upheld by the unanimous agreement of nations if it finds a means of realising what they are all awaiting, if it can contribute to put a stop, by the mere effort of reason, to a state of affairs which can no longer continue.

Your reporter feels himself honoured in having been entrusted with setting forth the data of the problem, and he eagerly submits to the attention of his colleagues of all nationalities, the arguments and the facts which he has already on many occasions brought to the notice of the French Parliament.

There exists, nevertheless, a great difference between the powers of a national parliament (where each member, responsible for his votes, is invested by the constitution with an authority which determines the measure of his action) and the weakness of a self-constituted assembly such as ours, which runs the risk of manifesting its good will without effect, since it is without control and without mandate. Let us, therefore, before all, seek a means of giving legality to our existence, or at least a sanction to our labours. That is our first duty. Perhaps the simplest means would be for each of us to obtain a mandate from the parliament of which he is a member, and to which he would have to render an account on his return. What is certain is, that the international discussion opened by us to-day, will be all the more fruitful in results in proportion as the national echo, which it will have in each of our countries, is assured.

The Conquest of National Opinion.
Patriotism.

In default of an organisation which it is impossible to improvise, let us at least seek support in the force that is at our service, namely, that of public opinion. Let us be its interpreters. It will support us. It is ready and has been tested. The progress realised in the domain of Arbitration within the last few years, with the assistance of public opinion, shows us what we can obtain in the domain of the limitation of armaments, which is infinitely more concrete and simple.

In 1899 the idea of international justice took shape in the form of a permanent Court of Arbitration. Unappreciated at first, boycotted from the beginning, the Hague Tribunal has been saved by the initiative of the United States, which is, *par excellence*, the country of public opinion. It triumphed in 1902, thanks to President Roosevelt. Two years later the normal recourse to the new jurisdiction having become habitual, it arrested a conflict which was imminent on the high seas between the British and Russian fleets. On that day the sophism of inevitable conflagrations received a blow strong enough to counterbalance the effect of the Russo-Japanese war upon public opinion. The application of The Hague conventions appeared to be, if not certainly a panacea, at least a great resource. Governments ceased to see in them a palliative or seeming remedy reserved solely for unimportant differences. Is it not also permissible to see in the Conference of Algeciras a conciliation preventive of one of those inextricable difficulties which, in a general way, can only be touched by war, and which would afterwards be relegated to diplomacy to repair the evil done—but after what sacrifices and what hecatombs? Finally, shall we not take into acount all the initiative, private and even official, which has arisen in all directions in favour of a pacific propaganda, of a second Hague Conference, of a permanent representation of the nations, and of the creation, even at this late hour, of a general international demonstration?

And how can one be astonished at these numerous symptoms and fortunate results? How can nations delay the organisation of order and justice in their relations, when each day they spontaneously discover so many manifestations of natural solidarities in their common activities? The more science and education awakens in them the idea of their respective interests, the more will they seek to reconcile these interests, and will feel repugnance against adventures Thus public opinion shows us the necessity of the new organisation. It impels us towards this progress which our intellectual indolence is disposed to regard as a paradox, but which is nevertheless very real, namely, that arising from the solidarity of patriotisms, a solidarity which will necessarily end in co-operation and in the association of nations.

It is true that this co-operation is not easy to realise, especially in Europe, with her ancient institutions, but we are nevertheless marching in that direction. We have already tried it on several occasions, in the case of *force majeure* in the East, and in the Far East, and these attempts are daily becoming more regular. They are essential, in order to secure the inter-communication of peoples, and to solve the thousand problems arising from the discoveries of science, the development of commerce and industry, the exigencies of parliamentary representation, and the necessity of levelling, without too much inequality, in all civilised countries, the moral and material conditions of human existence. Why should not the old world profit by the example of the new? The Conference of Rio de Janeiro, which has officially assembled across the ocean at the same time that we are sitting in London, offers a model of organisation that is wanting in Europe. Each state of the three Americas has certainly its domestic and foreign difficulties, but none of them has hesitated to make sacrifices for the conquest of its independence. All of them have, however, understood that the surest means of maintaining this independence was not by mistrust and excess of armaments but by agreement. None of them thinks of abdicating any part of its individuality. Many of them have solved the problem of the concerted reduction of armaments, and there is an understanding amongst them all to study together questions of common interest.

I admit that this generation of Europeans, brought up in traditions of antagonism anterior to the introduction of steam and electricity, has some difficulty in enlarging its conceptions of international relations, and is troubled with respectable, though unjustifiable, scruples; but the new generations, no longer recognising distance, will liberate themselves from the prejudices which separate different peoples. They look to us for guidance. Let us not hesitate to give it to them. Let us understand each other in order to begin work on our return to our respective countries. Let us not have any illusions. Here all of us can form our convictions, but it is not here that we must act. It is, furthermore and above all, necessary that all of us should do our duty in our own countries, where we must persuade, convert, combat. In a word, we must fulfil our national duty. That is everything. However beneficial may be our international manifestations, they are only an echo or a signal : our Inter-parliamentary Union will only be really effective in proportion to the various national actions of which it will be the consummation. International action is the aim; national action is the means. In a word, the value of the international organisation will be equivalent to that of our respective national organisations.

That is a fact of which you will find a striking proof in the assistance given to our ideas by the most liberal nations, large and small. Their services are in proportion to the liberalism of their institutions, and our progress is in proportion to their aid.

In support of this vital argument I will cite the example of France, which has been transformed in thirty-six years. But even this transformation has only become definitive under the impulse of a methodical and incessant propaganda, starting from the day that a certain number of Frenchmen understood that there was no hope of improving international relations and solving international problems without commencing to modify the national spirit which had been wilfully falsified and obscured. For that purpose it was necessary to have a new school, and to awaken a new conscience; it was necessary, in a word, to undertake a struggle against national error, which is the basis of international conflicts.

My friends and myself who are here have taken a part in this struggle that is smaller than we could have wished, and we take care not to forget those who have preceded us and given the example, and particularly those who have died in harness, succumbing under insults and attacks but falling victorious. Each has done what was in his power, but each of us knew that nothing of what we had secured in the international sphere would have been gained without an ardent co-operation in the work of national education. Thus we regret nothing of these struggles, nothing of the outrages that have been daily heaped upon us; we even consider that our continual combats are necessary for arousing the sympathies of public opinion. In reality the principal difficulties of our campaign have not been, and are not, the obstacles raised by our adversaries. Everything taken into account, our adversaries have served us by the too evident injustice and violence of their accusations. No; the real difficulties were the scruples of our friends.

Nowhere, I believe, has the campaign for Arbitration and the limitation of armaments been more strenuously opposed than in France, and nowhere, on the other hand, has it met with scruples more respectable or more worthy of consideration. I ought to speak of these scruples because they are human as well as national. Besides, you may be sure that if we in France have been able to answer them to the satisfaction of our consciences, you will easily succeed in overcoming them everywhere else,

and limitation will, before long, have in its favour
the unanimity of governments, because it will have
for it the unanimity of peoples.

Many of my friends who follow my campaign
with uneasiness do not recognise its patriotic character. They see in it on the contrary a blunder and
a danger. I do not, of course, refer to exaggerations,
or to the stupidities which are attributed to us. We
no longer reply to those who confound our efforts to
render Arbitration general, and to bring about a
simultaneous limitation of armaments, with I do not
know what dreams of disarmament and universal
peace. I thus sum up what has been said to me a
thousand times :—

_ " Nothing is more praiseworthy than a campaign
in favour of Arbitration and the limitation of
armaments, but is it in France that it should commence? Is it fitting for conquered and mutilated
France to preach Peace? Address yourselves first
to her conquerors, if you can secure a hearing.
Take care, however, in the interests of justice and
liberty themselves, not to weaken in France the
energy indispensable for the defence of your principles. If France is, unfortunately, the only
country to understand you, and if you naively allow
the spirit of conquest to dominate in the surrounding nations, take care lest you might awaken among
them not emulation but temptation. Take care
lest you make of France, not an example but a prey,
and thus let loose upon the world a universal
war."

This is the objection. It is a grave problem which
it would be puerile or criminal to pretend to evade.

It is true that republican France is obliged to be

particularly circumspect. If the pacific propaganda implies that she repudiates her immutable devotion to justice; if the pacific propaganda implies, as has been said, that every Frenchman should convert himself into a sheep in order to bleat a supplication for Peace before adversaries hostile to all spirit of conciliation and mutual concessions, then, as I have declared on' many occasions, I should be ashamed of it. I should be ashamed of it for my own name and for my children. That propaganda would be fatal for France, for freedom, for civilisation, and would result in the most demoralising consecration of violence; but such a propaganda is not that of any Frenchman. Do not listen to the calumnies of party spirit. No honest man is taken in by them. We are not cowards. It appears to us that we have proved our courage in defying prejudice and interested clamours, and we should, if necessary for the triumph of our ideas, willingly prove it again, not by words, but with our blood.

No; our campaign for Peace is a form, and a higher form, of patriotism.

The school of truth, which contemporary France seeks to establish, prepares men, initiative, and energies a hundred times more valuable in the day of danger than the superannuated and equivocal traditions of militarism. Since when has the teaching of liberty led to slavery? And how can we suppose that a nation which realises the supreme effort of self-direction can at the same time neglect to defend herself? Only those who endeavour to discredit our regime could think it capable of such an absurd contradiction.

No; France, on the contrary, like all laborious nations, develops its strength in Peace while reducing to a minimum the risks of conflict. The greater her attachment to progress, to the conquest of her independence and of her labour, the more reason will she have for defending these conquests and the greater will be her means for successfully doing so. Yes; the greater will be her means, because in increasing the number of her friends and of her customers she increases the volume of her resources. One might even say that she draws from her good foreign relations a large part of the resources necessary for her national defence. All these go together. France has only been really weak when she has been a source of anxiety for the world, and that is the history of all aggressive States. Since she has become pacific she is strong in general sympathy, while at the same time her prosperity has increased. We had experience of this thirty-six years ago, when Chauvinistic France was isolated. To-day she counts as many friends as she had formerly enemies. What changes! And who will maintain that our army, our navy, our colonies, as well as our agriculture, our industry and our commerce do not derive from them the most evident advantage.

Therefore the patriotic scruple that has been raised against us turns in our favour. France has every interest in favouring a pacific policy which will benefit herself as well as other countries. She will thus remain faithful to her intellectual and moral mission in propagating a great idea, and the whole world, beginning with the French themselves, will be grateful to her for fulfilling that mission. This has been clearly proved by events. And it is not blindly that, in reply to the violent attacks of which we have been the object, the Departmental Councils of France, as well as the Chambers of Commerce, voted addresses of sympathy with our Parliamentary Group for the Promotion of Arbitration. Nor is it without motive that the number of representatives of different countries, who have joined our institution, exceed 400. The conquest of the French national opinion to our ideas is an accomplished fact.

THE ATTITUDE OF THE POWERS AND THEIR INTEREST.

That much being said, the patriotic scruple has all the less reason to exist in France, seeing that our Government is not called upon to consider whether it should, or should not, take the initiative in proposing the limitation of armaments. That initiative has been taken. It has been taken, indeed, ten times over in categorical terms. It has, however, always met with the most discouraging reception. Under the pretext of patriotism a number of governments have obstinately closed their ears to successive appeals that have reached them from all quarters. Let us enumerate these appeals and ask ourselves what future generations, who will have to bear the burden of our debts, will think of such incapacity to come to a decision.

RUSSIA.

The Russian Government proposed, on August 24th, 1898, with a view to the requirements of her economic expansion, that a Conference on *Disarma-*

ment should be held. That was the first official title, afterwards changed to that of the *Peace Conference.* The terms of this proposal were so formal, and so pressing, that they stirred the world with a sort of electric shock.

I proposed to read to you the text of Count Mouravieff's celebrated circular, and to ask whether the most exacting amongst us had ever raised a stronger protest, but the British Prime Minister yesterday forestalled me, in the admirable speech which we have all applauded, a speech for which we all thank Sir Henry Campbell-Bannerman, because it implied an act of faith and of courage, because it is for us the most precious recompense and the most signal encouragement. I will, however, read you some extracts from Count Mouravieff's circular :—

" The maintenance of general Peace and a possible reduction of excessive armaments, which burden all nations, presents itself to us as an ideal towards which the efforts of all governments should be directed.

" In its conviction that this elevated aim responds to the most essential interests and legitimate aspirations of all the Powers, the Imperial Government believes that the present moment would be very favourable for seeking, by an international discussion, the most efficacious means of assuring to all the nations the benefits of a real and durable peace, *and, above all, of putting a limit to the present progressive development of armaments.*

" Financial burdens which are increasing affect public prosperity at its source. The intellectual and physical energies of peoples, as well as labour and capital, are for the most part diverted from their natural application and unproductively consumed. Hundreds of millions are employed in acquiring frightful engines of destruction, which are considered to-day as the aim of scientific invention, but to-morrow are destined to become valueless in consequence of some new discovery in the same domain. National culture, economic progress, and the production of wealth are paralysed or warped in their development.

" Furthermore, in proportion as the armaments of each Power increase, they respond less and less to the end which the governments had in view. The economic crises, due in a great measure to the regime of armaments *à outrance*, and the continual danger which lies in this heaping up of war material transforms the armed Peace of our time into a crushing burden which peoples find it harder and harder to bear. *It therefore appears evident that if this state of things is prolonged it will inevitably lead to precisely that cataclysm which we seek to avert, the thought of the horrors of which causes the human mind to shudder.*

" To put an end to these incessant armaments, and to seek a means of averting the calamities which threaten the whole world, is the supreme duty which to-day imposes itself on all States."

It is true, as the sceptics tell us, that since the Mouravieff circular war has broken out, followed by revolution, its habitual attendant. ' But the result of this contradiction of excellent intentions imposed by an unfortunate policy has proved more forcibly than any diplomatic circular how much Russia has lost by departing from these intentions.

At all events, the Duma, whose representatives

we yesterday acclaimed in this hall, have adopted as their own the Imperial decision. Our friends from St. Petersburg have corresponded with the French Parliamentary Group for the Promotion of Arbitration; they have considered its progress, studied its organisation, and, in response to our appeal, one of the first manifestations of their activity has been to establish a group similar to the French one. They have come to London to enrich the Inter-parliamentary Union by the infusion of new blood, but young and full of promise. They have come to realise at the first stroke what is now the hope, and what will soon be the programme, of the Union. They have come not, like the rest of us, simple, voluntary scouts, but as representatives and delegates of their parliament, whose mission is to bring us a new force, and with power to secure at home the adoption of the resolutions taken here.

It is true that circumstances will not permit them completely to fulfil their mandate, the dissolution of the Duma intervening as one more contradiction; but the double fact nevertheless remains that the Russian Government first, and the Russian Parliament afterwards, have pronounced themselves, in irrevocable terms, in favour of our ideas.

GREAT BRITAIN.

Has the Russian initiative in favour of the limitation of armaments remained isolated? Has it only held the ludicrous morrow of war? No; it has not prevented war, any more than the existence of madness and crime can be prevented by any prudent measures; but it has found an echo, and has been taken up by other countries. In the first place, Great Britain has taken a clear stand, and, as always happens in this country with a truly parliamentary regime, it is to Parliament that the Government has made known its views. It was to the House of Commons that Mr. Goschen, then First Lord of the Admiralty, made the following declaration, on March 9th, 1899 :—

" We are ready to reduce or modify our programme of new construction and to maintain the existing proportions. We have not accelerated the movement of construction, we have only followed it. But I declare, in the name of Her Majesty's Government, that if the other Great Powers are disposed to restrict their programmes of construction, we are ready for our part to enter into this course with them, and to modify our own. It is certain that the difficulties of such an agreement will be immense, but we are sincerely desirous of seeing the Conference lighten the terrible burden which weighs upon the nations of Europe."

And Mr. Goschen completed his declaration by the following announcement :—

" If this agreement is not arrived at we shall then adhere to the programme which I lay before the House."

What consequence followed this declaration? None. Diplomacy ignored it, treating it as a dead letter. That is the fate of the majority of new initiatives, but the initiative nevertheless exists. The most adverse circumstances have not been able to prevent the lassitude manifested in 1899 being much less justified in 1906, after seven years of redoubled sacrifices. It has been said, in order to explain these formidable increases in naval and military ' expenditure; exactly coinciding with government\ declarations condemning them, that there was no great merit in England accepting a general arrest of this expenditure, and particularly that on the navy, since this arrest would have no other effect than to assure to her the benefit of the large advance she has already secured over the other Powers. But this shows the absurdity of our general tendency. Each increases its sacrifices at the same time in order not to allow itself to be surpassed, therefore the distance between all the rival Powers remains the same, the proportion does not vary. None of them will emerge strengthened by this rivalry, and ruin awaits them all.

One shudders at thinking that if, during the past ten years, the Powers had come to an understanding to moderate their pace they would have saved milliards, from which progress would have benefited, without any modification of their respective positions. They would simply be richer, and their political embarrassments would not be so great.

Nevertheless, after Lord Goschen and the Marquis of Salisbury, then Prime Minister, there is a long list of English statesmen who have expressed their opinion in favour of a limitation of armaments, from Mr. J. Chamberlain, in 1903, to the present Liberal Prime Minister. Mr. J. Chamberlain spoke and wrote, in 1903, in the name of the Unionist Conservative Government, of which he was a member. I have many times cited these statements, particularly in the French Senate on April 11th, 1905, and April 9th, 1906, and in an open letter to

M. Delcassé, on August 3rd, 1903. Lord Lansdowne himself has not failed to declare that the
present situation is *intolerable*, and that he and all
his colleagues would approve of any serious attempt
that might be made in favour of a reduction of the
colossal expenditure which weighs upon the great
Powers (*Sitting of the House of Lords, May 25th,
1905*). He even claims, and justly, for his party
and his Government, the honour of having, in fact,
already entered on this path. Sir Henry Campbell-
Bannerman, with his habitual loyalty, recognised
this fact when speaking to you yesterday.

Lord Lansdowne did not mean by that to expose
his country to the risks of an attack—and no one
in England, any more than elsewhere, has ever
imagined a limitation of armaments leading to the
destruction of the equilibrium of international forces
for the profit of one or more States against others—
but he said and repeated :—

" It would in our eyes be an admirable thing if,
by a common agreement, we could succeed in
reducing those sacrifices " (*May 22nd, 1906*).
These words in the mouth of a man who has done
so much for the Peace of the world, and who has
acquired for himself, we may say, without distinction of country or party, general esteem and confidence, these words, which my honourable friend
Arthur Balfour will not deny, ought to have in our
eyes an encouraging significance. The language of
Sir Edward Grey, the worthy successor of Lord
Lansdowne at the Foreign Office, is still more
categorical.

At the end of last year (December 22nd, 1905)
Sir Henry Campbell-Bannerman had already said :—

"We Liberals do not forget that we are the heirs to a great and noble tradition. This tradition was born in the days when public opinion was opposed to all attempts to settle differences by an appeal to reason and to the conscience of humanity.

"Mr. Gladstone defied the public opinion of his time. He placed himself upon a more elevated plane, and in referring the *Alabama* dispute to Arbitration he established a precedent of incalculable value for humanity.

"I rejoice that since that period the principle of Arbitration has made great progress, and that to-day it is no longer regarded as a weakness on the part of any of the Great Powers of the world to submit to a higher tribunal those differences which were formerly settled by force.

"Ah! gentlemen, it is useless to seek Peace if you do not act logically. I consider that the increase of armaments is a great danger for the Peace of the world.

"A policy of enormous armaments upholds and promotes the idea that force is the first, if not the only, solution of international differences.

"It is a policy which tends to re-open old sores and provoke new wounds. It being granted that the principle of pacific Arbitration is making progress, one of the noblest tasks for statesmen consists in modifying those armaments in view of a new and happier era.

"Is there a more noble rôle for this great country than, at the present moment, to place herself at the head of a League of Peace, through the intermediation of which this work might be accomplished?

"We want," concluded Sir Henry Campbell-

Bannerman, "to lighten the burden of excessive taxation, and at the same time we lack the money necessary for arriving at this desirable end if, in time of Peace, our armaments are maintained on a war footing. Do not think of this madness which causes us to be called Little Englanders. I am at least patriotic enough not to wish to see my country weakened by a waste such as that of the past ten years."

In his turn, Sir Edward Grey, Minister for Foreign Affairs, has emphatically confirmed the declarations of the Prime Minister. You will remember the motion of our colleague, Mr. Vivian, in the House of Commons, in favour of a study of the limitation of armaments," to be concerted between England and the other Powers. This motion has, since May 25th, been supported by our eminent friend Lord Avebury, and also by Lord Edmund Fitzmaurice, in the House of Lords. In the House of Commons it was welcomed by Sir Edward Grey in the following words, which were loudly applauded (May 10th):—

"The national expenses have enormously increased in recent years. It is possible to reduce them without sacrificing the security of the country.

"I approve of the resolution proposed by Mr. Vivian because of the effect it might have in other countries. At no time has public opinion in Europe pronounced itself more strongly in favour of Peace, and yet the burden of military and naval expenditure has not ceased to increase. The Hague Conference could not render the world any greater service than in making the conditions of Peace less expensive.

"It is said that we wait for foreign Powers to take the initiative before reducing our expenditure. In reality the Powers are all waiting for each other. Some day or another it will be necessary for one of them to take the first step.

"It is possible that another Power may be ready to take the initiative, but nothing ought to prevent us from doing so.

"In the name of the Government I accept and welcome Mr. Vivian's motion, and I hope that the Powers will consider it as an invitation from the English Government to respond to an appeal in favour of the reduction of armaments."

ITALY.

We are thus clearly acquainted with the views of Great Britain and Russia. Let us continue our inquiry methodically. Let us realise the irresistible force of a sound idea, the happy contagion of a beneficent initiative. The germ of this initiative exists in every mind, but it is dormant. The first time it shows itself everything seems to conspire to discourage it, but it persists; it weakens the mistrust that surrounds it, afterwards winning attention and, finally, sympathy.

Hardly had Mr. Vivian's motion called forth a response and a favourable vote in the British Parliament when another of our colleagues, M. Brunialti, in another parliament not less animated than that of London with a generous mission for Peace, the Parliament of Rome, gave the Italian Government an opportunity of declaring itself in turn (June

14th). M. Tittoni, Minister for Foreign Affairs, far from seeking to evade the question, replied, amidst great attention, in the most unconditionally favourable terms, of which the following is a résumé :—

"To-day, as the Italian Minister for Foreign Affairs, I publicly express the adhesion of the Government to the humanitarian ideas which found in the historic Hall of Westminster an ample and authorised assent. I have always considered that it would be a crime of high treason to our country for us alone to weaken our armaments while we found ourselves in the midst of a Europe powerfully armed, and which considers the perfecting of armaments as a guarantee of Peace.

"I am, however, equally of opinion that it would be high treason against humanity not to co-operate in initiatives having for their object the simultaneous reduction of the armaments of the Great Powers. Italian policy has always aimed at the maintenance of Peace, consequently I am happy to be able to inform the honourable M. Brunialti that our delegates at the approaching Conference at The Hague will have a mandate to support the English initiative."

It must, moreover, be observed that in these declarations the Italian Minister, while accepting the principle of limitation and even, it has since been said, the principle of the reduction of military expenditure, spoke in the interests of the army, and in agreement with the higher technical authorities. That is one of the results of Chauvinistic delirium in all countries. The megalomaniacs finish by disquieting not only the taxpayers and all the productive forces which they exhaust, but even the

most eminent personalities of the army and the
navy. You would not have to make very long investigation to discover around you a number of
naval and military officers thoroughly hostile to the
waste from which they know well the national
defence would finally suffer much more than it
would benefit. They deplore that, under the pretext of constantly modifying an instrument already
too complicated and too often renewed, artificial
industries are created which exist to the detriment
of the natural activity of the country. They deplore that under the pretext of strengthening the
army and the navy they are being paralysed.

The unrestricted increase in the tonnage of ironclads, for example, and the range of cannon have
arrived at a point constituting a sort of game which
gives the impression of an unhealthy aberration or
a mystification. It is impossible not to realise that
even those who blame us, in the name of patriotism,
for organising good international relations do not
fail to internationalise the waste by which they
profit. Let them beware: their excess of zeal is
becoming suspicious. One will soon see in it not
the expression, but the international exploitation, of
patriotism.

FRANCE.

I recognise and deplore the fact that the French
Government has been more reserved than the
Russian, British and Italian Governments, but it
has had more than one excuse to justify this reserve,
and my honourable colleague, M. Messimy, Reporter
on the Budget in the French Chamber of Deputies,

will, doubtless, tell you, as he has recently demonstrated to our Arbitration Group, that France is relatively less unreasonable than the other Powers as far as military expenditure is concerned. However that may be, the declarations of the French Government have been up to the present very vague. One might even say that in spite of the progress of our ideas they have, until recently, been purely dilatory. Some weeks ago, however, we had the satisfaction of hearing, in reply to pressing questions, the present Minister declare that he also would welcome with sympathy every initiative in favour of an international study of the limitation of armaments. Our Minister for Foreign Affairs, M. Leon Bourgeois, my former colleague at The Hague Conference, has not forgotten the part he then took in the drawing up of a motion which was voted unanimously, and the text of which is known to you :—

"The Conference considers that the progressive limitation of armaments, which at the present time weigh so heavily on the world, is extremely desirable for the development of the moral and material welfare of humanity."

The Ministerial declaration of June 12th, 1906, has revived this affirmation.

JAPAN. AUSTRALIA. CHINA.

Will the armaments that are being developed outside Europe, the victories of Japan, even the projects of China, and those of Australia, as well as the expenditure of the United States, be invoked

against our contention? I will reply that it is quite
true that militarism tends to develop itself everywhere in the wake of Europe, and that if Europe
decided to give a better example, all the world would
be thankful for it, and would reckon with it., It is
in vain for Europe to try and fix upon new peoples
responsibility for the evils she herself has let loose,
and the cessation of which depend upon her.

The military strength of Japan is a European
creation. Japan has nothing to gain and all to lose
by developing it beyond measure. Her vital interest
is to limit her expenditure for defensive organisation
to the lowest level. It is contrary to her interest to
momentarily abandon herself to the trial of monster
ironclads; but she has proved that she knows how
to emancipate herself from our exaggerations, and
this experience will perhaps contribute, still more
than our errors, in opening her eyes, and in bringing
her back to her admirable rule of the maximum
of effect at the minimum of expenditure.

Australia, too, in the midst of people armed to
the teeth, could not escape from the necessity of
defending herself; but it is in that country, *par
excellence*, that the incompatibility between the
cost of armed Peace and social expenditure becomes
obvious.

Australia could not be at the same time a field
of experiment for the reforms of our epoch and the
barren ground for the manœuvres of militarism.
She is, therefore, entirely in favour of the limitation
of armaments. She could not sacrifice her work of
colonisation to military service. The hands at her
disposal are not numerous enough. The recruiting
of a permanent army and navy in a country in the

course of formation is a veritable anomaly and a
cause of frustration and ruin.

It is entirely different with China, that in-
exhaustible reservoir of men. There, while the
white Great Powers continue their mad rivalry,
nothing will be easier than to follow them, and
even surpass them; but there again the Yellow
Peril, which is scoffed at, will be our own work.
Civilisation can avoid it or create it, according as
it performs or fails to perform its duty. Already it
has provoked many evils which are difficult to
remedy, commencing with the hatred of the
foreigner, insurrections and massacres. In China,
as in Turkey, as in all the States of the East, and
the Far East, militarism is but a European importa-
tion, the caricature of our own exaggerations. It
is we who encourage and sometimes even oblige
these governments, who are too weak to resist us,
to buy from us ironclads and cannon which they do
not know what to do with, if not to turn against
their own subjects, against their neighbours, and,
finally, against us.

THE UNITED STATES.

America requires special treatment. I must
excuse myself for the development of this study, but
it is as complex as it is urgent, and your confidence,
as well as the importance of the subject, forbids
me to treat it too incompletely.

For some time past the situation of the United
States has furnished for international Chauvinism
a number of fresh arguments, each more superficial
than the others, which have been abused by our

megalomaniacs. Just as they ignore the immense economy secured in the Japanese military organisation, and grossly misrepresent the lessons of the battle of Tsushima, in order to support their demands for fresh expenditure, they see in the incontestable growth of the military expenditure of the United States only a pretext for increasing those of other countries. It is a profound error. The United States consent, it is true, to great sacrifices for the maintenance of relatively small forces, but that is exactly a sign of their natural inaptitude for militarism. If militarism were normal in their country the soldiers would cost less. But how is it possible to constitute a permanent army, an army of Peace, an idle army, in a country in the course of formation, where no one has leisure, where everybody works, where wages are high, and where there is a constant lack of manual labour? That army would be a veritable defiance to the good sense and the patriotism of the nation. The ideal of a democratic state is that every one should be at work in times of Peace, and every one under arms in time of war. As, however, the United States, in the present condition of the world, can not be the only disarmed Power, they are obliged to take their precautions against the abuse of militarism by others, and as, after all, they themselves are not able to escape the effect of our example, it follows that they also have an army, the smallest army possible; and it is only natural that this small army should be more expensive than all the rest; but then who will venture to compare their army with that of any European State? Travelling from New York to

Chicago I do not remember having met with a single American soldier in the course of six weeks. We thus realise that the United States can form but a small army at great expense, and that expense is an argument in favour of our contention and not against it.

I would say the same of the American navy. I admit that the military metal industry exercises its influence there as elsewhere. Protection has everywhere the inevitable corollary of this further premium for national industry—military contracts. But it is not enough to order ironclads; crews must also be provided; and then the problem is the same as for the army—you cannot enlist foreign sailors, and there is not sufficient national labour. Notwithstanding everything, the Americans will have a navy, but it is we Europeans who will have forced them to it, as we have forced the Japanese; and yet they will have, by the force of circumstances, not the largest but the smallest possible navy, and that precisely because it will be the most costly. Such are the exact words used by Mr. Charles Bonaparte, Secretary for the Navy, in his annual report for 1905, page 23. However small it may be, it will necessarily be in proportion to the extent of their coast, their immense territory, and their large population. The United States cannot fairly be compared to this or that European Power; the comparison must be with the whole of Europe. If, for instance, we proceed to compare the American navy with that of France, which is frequently done in our country, it follows that with 80,000,000 of inhabitants the American navy must in the course of time exceed that of France, whose population is only 38,000,000. That is a mathematical certainty. Consequently, we Frenchmen have the greatest interest not to engage in this match with America, in which we should be sure to be beaten. The same reasoning holds good for Germany, although she has a population superior to that of France by one-third.

The United States do not want an army. They know perfectly well that their geographical position renders them unassailable. Their whole effort will, therefore, be directed to the firm organisation of the naval forces necessary for victoriously resisting any mad European enterprise. This organisation, thanks to submersibles, torpedo boats, coast defence and wireless telegraph, will from day to day be more effective and less costly. The time approaches —if it has not already arrived—when it will be impossible and absurd to send out a European squadron against any of the confederated American States. The converse, however, is not completely true, if Europe remains divided, and if one of its States, acting contrary to another, offers the shelter of its ports to the American navy. In any case, Germany, differing in that respect from the United States, is obliged to divide its forces between sea and land, or rather she ought to double them in order to be able to oppose at the same time the largest army in the world next to her own, and the largest navy. That is doubly exhausting and always deceptive, because, once entered upon this path, we are no longer masters of our hypothesis. It is always possible to suppose that the strongest army in the world, after that of Germany, and the strongest navy could one day join hands with another army and another navy; the French army, for instance, with the English army, and the English navy with the Japanese. American or Australian navies, or even with all the other navies. Thus the most unrestricted expenditure and sacrifices could not give to Germany any more than to any other Power the certainty of military superiority, a fact which demonstrates the illusory character of this expenditure and those sacrifices.

No European nation can flatter itself with the hope of being alone able to check, surpass, or even equal, the development of the United States. Germany, as well as France, might exhaust itself in this enterprise, but we should only succeed in obliging the United States, notwithstanding their natural inaptitude, to concentrate at all costs upon their navy the constantly increasing strength of their resources and their population. We shall oblige them to divert that effort from the work of Peace to devote it to the work of war. They would not forgive us, and we should gain nothing by it— France not being able to follow for want of population, nor Germany for want of money. But do people not believe that popular discontent will one day or other oppose a resistance to this game? . . .

Let us resign ourselves, therefore, to accept the dictates of common sense. Let us not attempt to enter upon a rivalry with the United States, which would be disastrous for them as well as for us. Their navy will be that of a great country, that is inevitable, as is proved by the vigorous campaign of Captain Hobson, but thanks to progress it can be infinitely simplified and be very different to ours. They do not hold with following us in our errors. They do not hold with constructing costly arsenals to be encumbered with colossal material which becomes old-fashioned quicker than it can be produced. They will in this way, as in their agricultural enterprises, find the necessary simplifications. They will not be simple enough to borrow from us, for the first time, that which is most doubtful and ephemeral in our old systems. The exigencies of their economic and social development will, on the contrary, furnish them with the means for making use of everything that is most modern in our discoveries. In a word, they will surpass us with our and their own inventions, and not with our routine, and that is why it is puerile to force their pace by hastening our own. They will be happy to join the Powers favourable to limitation of armaments, and even to encourage them. On this point I have referred to the declarations of the present Secretary of State for the Navy, Mr. Charles Bonaparte. President Roosevelt has not been less clear in his recent Message (December, 1905), which is singularly in agreement with our contention, and of which, on April 9th last, I quoted the following extract in the French Senate:—

" We shall by degrees make a step in advance in order to arrive at something like an organisation of the civilised States, for this reason, that the more the world attains a higher organisation the less will be the needs for navies and armies.

" Immediate disarmament is impossible — that would be an encouragement for the noxious States— but it may be possible to check the tendency to the indefinite increase of war budgets.

" Of course, only reasonable efforts in this direction can succeed."

The President of the United States is no more disposed than ourselves to abandon his country to the cupidity of an invader, but he does not hesitate to advocate a new organisation, and in the meanwhile he echoes the Russian, English, Italian and French declarations in favour of limitation. Let us note this symptom. Let us not diminish its considerable significance. Let us not forget that the more a State is embarrassed in keeping up with this rivalry in armaments—even though its resources may be immense—the more it becomes difficult for its government to declare it too openly, and the more it should fear that its manifestation of wisdom may not be an encouragement for the errors of others.

The New World : The Small Powers.

Besides, President Roosevelt is not the only interpreter of the feelings of the United States. No; all America, the whole of the New World, expresses the same opinion—the Republic of Mexico, the first, with the United States, that dared to unbewitch the Hague Tribunal; Brazil, which has given us the example of including compulsory Arbitration in its constitution; the Argentine Republic, and Chili. Nevertheless, the too persuasive eloquence of the European metal industry made itself felt there as elsewhere. There national antagonisms, apparently irreconcilable, seem always ready to deluge the frontiers of these peoples with blood; there the disorder caused by rival ambitions, the temptation of wealth to be conquered, and the difficulty of creating political organisations—there, more than anywhere else, these constitute a continual danger of conflict. It is there, nevertheless, that we see the signature of the first convention for the reduction of armaments, as also the first general convention for Arbitration. I remember the weight given in our deliberations at The Hague to the example afforded in 1898 by the Argentine Republic signing with Italy its famous Treaty of Arbitration, and how proud of this precedent was my eminent friend Count Nigra on behalf of his country. The young American Republic has not stopped there. Why should the wisdom, of which she afterwards gave evidence by reducing, in agreement with Chili, the number of her ironclads, fail to have influence on this occasion? These reductions have been passionately discussed at length by men of the highest intellectual and moral standing. They were voted because the Parliaments of Buenos Ayres and Santiago understood this simple truth, that two countries divided became weak in face of a third while increasing their rival forces, whereas, on the contrary, two countries united could reduce their forces and render them more formidable through their combination.

Let us not omit to add to the list of Powers which should be counted among the natural or declared partisans of limitation, those which a not very scientific tradition qualifies as small Powers, as if they were not capable of making themselves loudly heard and of setting us very great examples. Necessarily the small Powers are ardently desirous for the organisation of international justice from which they would be the first to profit. They are

still more anxious for the end of the regime of armed
Peace which has a ruinous reaction upon them, as
they are obliged, notwithstanding everything, to
arm themselves in order to exist in a continual state
of *qui vive*, and with the risk of complications that
constantly threaten their liberty and their existence,
which becomes all the more precarious as might
obstinately persists in denying right.

Germany. Austria-Hungary.

But what can I, as a Frenchman, say of
Germany?

I shall tell the truth to my German colleagues as
well as I have done to my French compatriots and
colleagues, because I shall speak without *arrière
pensée*, and with the certainty that the interest of
Germany is to limit her armaments at the same time
as the other Powers.

French Chauvinism and German Chauvinism
always in agreement are like all the Chauvinisms
in the world—detestable advisers. The discussion
between all the peoples of the world, which we open,
is, according to them, only a snare, a clumsy trap
in which we secretly hope that Germany will be
caught, willingly or by force. The French National-
ists have charitably warned me in their newspapers that my naive confidence will have a sanguin-
ary awakening, and that Germany, rather than
accept a forcible reduction of armaments, would
attack her neighbours, devouring some and taking
others as hostages, etc. The Germans, on the other
hand, write " that the military expenditure, how-

ever heavy it may be, constitutes the best investment, the wisest insurance against international
injustice, and that it would one day transform itself
into a profit." And that is why they add, " that the
enemies of Germany conspire against the increase
of this expenditure and the realisation of those advantages. They wish nothing less than to weaken
Germany. Germany is in their eyes already too
powerful. They are seeking to group themselves
against her, with a subtle patience and under the
mask of moderation more dangerous than direct
hostility; a positive coalition, renewing that which
overthrew Napoleon I. The project for the limitation of military and naval expenses is only an
expedient for securing the greatest possible limitation of the German forces, almost in the same way
as Napoleon I. limited the forces of the Prussian
army after Tilsit. What could be a better means
for France, England and the United States than to
counterbalance, by an international limitation of
armaments, the growth of population which an-
nually strengthens the German army? But in
Germany no one will be the dupe of such an
obvious machination. All patriots will understand
that the proposals for limitation had no other aim
but to put the axe to the German oak, and that the
answer of Germany to these proposals should be a
courteous refusal."

To these arguments I would, in the first place,
reply by this simple consideration : if it be true that
the limitation of armaments must be so highly pre-
judicial to Germany, how can it be explained that
the Chauvinists of other countries are nevertheless
the adversaries of this limitation? They ought to

be the first to demand it since they pretend that it is dreaded by Germany. Let us pass over this contradiction.

The question is to find out whether, yes or no, Germany has something to gain by making war. It is clear that she could only lose by it, and that even now by victories she would risk the raising up against herself of a natural coalition embracing a part of America and Asia. Therefore the object of her army is to maintain Peace, and her military budget is the insurance premium. If that be so the premium is excessive. It would be better to come to an understanding with her neighbours to secure a reduction of it. But how can it be contended that this military expenditure changes into a profit? We shall not be told, I suppose, as M. Brunetiere demonstrated in a masterly manner last year in the *Revue des Deux Mondes*, apropos of the French cavalry, that it is advantageous to employ the valour of German soldiers and the strength of their horses in exercises, and that Germany would be ruined if a portion of this valour and of those forces were applied to works of agriculture and industry. I, for my part, believe that the excess of her naval and military expenditure adds nothing to her security, nothing to her domestic prosperity, and nothing to her good foreign relations. I am convinced, on the contrary, that from the threefold standpoint, economic, social and political, the German Empire has the greatest interest in limiting the sacrifices which in a great measure paralyse her vitality and which in reality only serve to keep up a state of unrest. No one conspires against Germany. No one forms the puerile dream of hampering the development of a great race of which all the world admires the genius and recognises the future. It is possible momentarily to impede but not to prevent the growth of a race. That of Germany can only be hampered by excess of militarism and not by the machinations of her neighbours. The pressure of which she complains comes from her internal burdens and not from outside. The longer armed Peace is prolonged the greater will appear the interest of laborious and trading Germany, which will be contrary to the error of military Germany, and the more difficult it will be for her government to give a formal refusal to the desire for and the general need of a limitation of armaments.

For the rest, is it quite certain that Germany is determined to give a formal refusal? For my part I would not take upon myself the responsibility of saying that she is, and my opinion is based on recent experience.

I heard it contended in 1899 that her Government would not be represented at The Hague Conference. That was a mistake. Her delegates, like those of France, took part in our work. As was natural, they not only brought with them much circumspection, but also a strong desire to arrive at a conclusion. Without the goodwill of Count Münster, and the devotion of my friend Professor Zorn, the work of The Hague would have proved abortive, and the permanent Court of Arbitration would not have been created. Germany's two allies, Austria-Hungary and Italy, took an active part in that creation, and nobody appears to have had any ill-will towards them on that account. The German

Government finally signed and ratified the Conventions on July 29th, 1899.

But people will say that it did not show much eagerness to apply them. That is true, but I have made the same reproach a hundred times against the French Government. Does that justify despair?

It has also been said that the German Government would not follow the example given in the matter of Treaties of Arbitration. I heard this affirmed in July, 1904, and nevertheless at this same period the German and British Governments both felt so much the advantage of not resisting the pressure of general opinion that they agreed to sign one of those treaties.

Let us not forget that until three years ago all the world laughed at these treaties, and that to-day they are being signed on all hands. Why should it not be the same in the case of treaties of limitation?

Let us nevertheless recognise the fact that Germany, as compared with the other Powers, is. in a somewhat unpromising position for limiting her armaments. Her merchants, and not any longer her Chauvinists, raise this objection : " It is natural that certain Powers should have an interest in a general limitation—those whose population is small as, for example, France, or those who are already provided with colonies and have nothing further to conquer. Both have everything to gain by a consolidation of the present situation, which for them is equivalent to a privilege. But Germany is at the same time too populous and bereft of territories of expansion which the other Powers have reserved for themselves. Is that just? And if it be not just, can Germany resign herself to this injustice and wilfully close to her children the future that belongs to them in virtue of natural justice and in virtue of the old saying, 'All the world must live.' And even while admitting that the Germany of to-day may have the weakness to consecrate this injustice, who can undertake that these children will not later on revolt against the complaisance of a decision which would result in suicide for them? You see, therefore, that Germany cannot declare herself satisfied nor can she consequently enter a general association of the Powers disposed to limit their armaments.''

I will reply that no human association would be formed if a condition of its formation were the preliminary settlement of the wrongs or the removal of the inferiorities of each of its members. I will reply that France could also raise other and graver objections, and that she is not more free than Germany or any one else in the world to bind the consciences of future generations. But I will add that in this double fact, namely, that most of the Great Powers are satisfied with their colonial possessions and that Germany, on the contrary, is not satisfied, is precisely an element of agreement and not of conflict, and that this agreement might be realised by means of mutual and durable concessions if it were desired.

This arrangement will be the key to the organisation which is being developed in the sphere of morals before entering into that of fact, and the disorder of European colonisation will contribute in making its necessity felt.

The development of colonies is impossible under the regime of armed peace. Even their defence is more than hypothetical. Their security will not be complete until the day that submersibles shall have become sufficiently numerous and practicable to protect them. The idea of sending a sufficient number of ironclads to the Pacific to protect Indo-China, for example, against an attack by Japan, is not to be thought of; while with submarines and torpedo boats a defensive organisation is conceivable —on one condition, however, namely, that we have the co-operation of the natives. Now the burdens of armed Peace are such that the European Powers are obliged to grind down the natives even much more than the taxpayers of the Mother Country, and that, far from being able to count on their help, they have alienated them by their exactions.

The colonial policy of Europe will be transformed when in consequence of an international agreement these burdens shall become less heavy. The period of conquest having come to an end it will give place to a period of organisation and of civilisation in the true sense of the word. Until then European disorder will be aggravated by colonial disorder, and we shall see military expenditure increase, in times of perfect Peace in our distant possessions, as if a state of war were perpetuated there.

The Germans, it is true, will make the most of the fact that being the last to arrive at the division they are the worst served, *tarde venientibus ossa*, and that the colonial argument in favour of limitation has less weight in their councils than in those of the other Powers. But once more it is in this inequality that the remedy, the resource, is to be found. Who does not understand the grandeur of the rôle of the diplomacy of to-morrow. Who does not see its mission, its obvious duty? Armed Peace is no longer possible, war is no solution, and agreement alone can be efficacious. Routine and violence being powerless, it is for reason to decide.

BANKRUPTCY.

I think I have said enough on the subject, although it is so vast and demands much further development. I have said enough as to the attitude and the interests of all the Powers concerning the limitation of armaments. Others will complete this report, the summing up of my previous labours, and will further develop this sketch. I now come to deal with the motives which permit none of the Powers concerned to further postpone a solution. These motives may be summed up in one—the governments have no longer a choice. It is impossible to continue the present system. Only ten years hence people will be astonished that it could have lasted so long. However complicated it may appear, and in reality is, limitation is salvation, postponement is bankruptcy and revolution.

Bankruptcy? I will let the Ministers of our different countries speak on the subject. Not being able to quote them all I will take my figures from the present French Minister of Finance, M. Poincare, and I could add to his testimony that of most of his predecessors, M. Caillaux, M. Rouvier, and the principal Reporters of our Budgets both to the Senate and to the Chamber.

I will set forth in accordance with the statements of my French colleagues least open to the suspicion of Nationalism the general situation of the different budgets of the world, and M. Messimy will, for his part, say in what proportion, improbable but too true, the unproductive military expenditure has increased everywhere, and that, too, without altering the comparative strength of these budgets— a ridiculous and lamentable result for such a great effort.

Let us, however, bear in mind the difficulty of comparing budgets which are very differently drawn up. In this matter there are deceptive similarities which it is difficult to avoid, and, consequently, we must reconcile ourselves to great uncertainty on many points. We cannot any longer, even in France, compare our present budget with those of preceding periods. We now seem to bear a much heavier burden, but the increase is often only apparent, extraordinary expenditure which formerly escaped attention being to-day incorporated in our ordinary budget. In reality its incorporation simplified the budget. It constitutes a reform in the direction of sincerity. Account must also be taken of supplementary grants voted owing to insufficiency of receipts or reductions in taxation justifying equivalent increases in the expenditure.

In order to be able to compare the budgets of all countries it would be necessary that they should be equally sincere. In that respect also the national propaganda against national error should be the starting point of all international organisation.

If we, however, sum up in one round total all the expenditure of the same country we shall arrive at figures, not incontestable, but instructive, although only approximate. That is what M. Poincare has done. I take the following indications from his speech of April 8th, 1906, which the Senate ordered to be posted up in all the Communes of France.

The increase of expenditure is general. According to our Minister of Finance, that arises from the fact that many items of expenditure which had been dissimulated have become apparent, and to the further fact that there have been reductions of taxation so far as France is concerned. These figures might, therefore, be regarded as a sign of prosperity if the majority of them were for productive expenditure, but such is not the case.

Here is the table prepared by M. Poincare :—

GENERAL INCREASE IN BUDGETS FOR THE PAST TWENTY-SIX YEARS.

From 1880 to 1904 and 1905.

IN FRANCE (in millions of francs).

| For 1880 ... | ... | ... | ... | ... | ... | 3,378 |
| For 1905 ... | ... | ... | ... | ... | ... | 3,623 |

(We reach four milliards in the estimates for 1907.)

IN GERMANY (in thousands of marks). (Budget of the Empire.)

| For 1880 ... | ... | ... | ... | ... | ... | 550,065 |
| For 1905 ... | ... | ... | ... | ... | ... | 2,208,887 |

IN ENGLAND (in thousands of pounds sterling).

| For 1880 ... | ... | ... | ... | ... | ... | 82,108 |
| For 1904 ... | ... | ... | ... | ... | ... | 141,956 |

IN BELGIUM (in thousands of francs).

| For 1880 ... | ... | ... | ... | ... | ... | 292,010 |
| For 1905 ... | ... | ... | ... | ... | ... | 545,417 |

IN THE UNITED STATES (in thousands of dollars).

| For 1880 ... | ... | ... | ... | ... | ... | 267,643 |
| For 1904 ... | ... | ... | ... | ... | ... | 532,402 |

IN ITALY (in thousands of lires).

| For 1880 ... | ... | ... | ... | ... | ... | 1,196,678 |
| For 1905 ... | ... | ... | ... | ... | ... | 1,708,200 |

IN PRUSSIA (in thousands of marks).

For 1880	799,200
For 1904	2,803,800

IN RUSSIA (in millions of roubles).

For 1880	694
For 1905	1,916

Thus the approximate general increase of expenditure for the past 25 years is as follows:—

For France (francs)	244	millions
For Germany (marks)	1,658	,,
(About two milliards of francs.)		
For England (pounds sterling)... ...	59	,,
(1,475 million francs.)		
For Belgium (francs)	253	,,
For the United States (dollars) ...	265	,,
(1,300 million francs.)		
For Italy (lires)	512	,,
For Prussia (marks)	2,104	,,
(More than two and a-half milliards francs.)		
For Russia (roubles)	1,222	millions
(More than three milliards and a-half of francs.)		

Now turn to the proportion of unproductive expenditure in these increases.-

Such a table for all the Powers would lead me too far, and I will only refer to the figures of M. Messimy, but we shall be able to form an opinion of them from a single example, which, however, is one of the most moderate, namely, that of France.

Of our total expenditure of 3,623,000,000 francs in 1905 (now increased to 4,000,000,000 in the estimates for 1907) what is the annual proportion of unproductive expenditure? It is enormous.

There is first about a milliard to meet the interest on debts, for the most part representing military expenditure of the past.

Then come the expenses for the army, the navy and the colonies, amounting for the year 1905 to 1,260,000,000 francs. That is, more than 2,000,000,000 for unproductive expenditure.

So that out of a budget of 3,500,000,000 francs we have only an available balance of 1,500,000,000.

Nearly two-thirds of our budget is absorbed in war expenses.

The proportion in which these war expenses have increased far exceeds that of our productive expenditure.

In 1880 the War Expenses were ...	721	millions
Those of the Navy and the Colonies ...	200	„
Those of Pensions	100	„
Total	1,022	millions
War Expenses in 1905	690	millions
Naval and Colonial Expenses	400	„
Those for Pensions	170	„
Total	1,260	millions

The war expenses showed a slight decline in 1905, but only to increase the following year. The naval expenditure has, however, exactly doubled, increasing from 200,000,000 to 400,000,000 francs.

Military pensions in a period of absolute Peace have risen from 100,000,000 francs to 170,000,000.

Our Minister of Finance points out that during the past thirty-six years our military expenditure has attained the total of 42,000,000,000. He does not take into account the approximate sum of 30,000,000,000 for the interest on our debt, which makes a maximum total of 70,000,000,000 devoted to this unproductive expenditure. He does not, moreover, take into account the colossal loss of earnings represented by the time that 500,000 young men spend every year in barracks, which would amount to more than 15,000,000 men withdrawn for many years from the development of the country. It is difficult to imagine such a waste of resources and of strength. Let us really admire the patriotism and the vitality of a country capable of bearing it without complaint, but our admiration should be an additional motive for seeking to lighten its burden, for it is also necessary to think of the overwork, in addition to all the other plagues, which result from this infatuated expenditure in the social, moral and material order.

SCHEDULE OF THE EXPENDITURE AND OF THE MILITARY FORCES OF THE STATES OF EUROPE AND OF THE UNITED STATES OF AMERICA, 1905.

Country.	Men under arms.	Annual cost in Pounds sterling.
United States	107,000	40,000,000
Europe—		
United Kingdom	420,000	65,000,000
Russia	1,150,000	46,500,000
Germany	661,000	43,800,000
France	620,000	41,000,000
Austria-Hungary	384,000	19,000,000
Italy	305,900	17,000,000
Spain	100,000	6,700,000
Norway and Sweden	73,000	5,500,000
Turkey	370,000	4,800,000
Holland	35,000	3,650,000
Portugal	34,000	2,600,000
Belgium	50,000	2,500,000
Switzerland	148,000	1,300,000
Greece	23,000	1,200,000
Denmark	14,000	1,200,000
Bulgaria	43,000	1,000,000

So as not to take my figures from one source alone, and in order not to return to this point, I reproduce the above table prepared by Lord Avebury. It is a schedule of the expenditure of the military and naval forces of the States of Europe and of the United States of America in times of Peace. As far as Great Britain is concerned, Lord Avebury finds that the colossal figure of the expenditure—£65,000,000 (1,700,000,000 francs)—does not comprise the supplementary expenditure for fortifications and other works. On the other hand, in a recent discussion Sir Charles Dilke affirmed that a considerable amount of military expenditure is paid out of grants for the civil administration, for example, in Uganda, etc. This confirms the remark in which I have called attention to the impossibility of an exact comparison of the military expenditures of the world.

I have quoted Lord Avebury, a Member of the British Parliament and a savant whose authority is universally recognised. I could also quote among my friends, German, Italian, Norwegian, Dutch, Belgian, American and French savants, and not savants alone, nor philosophers; but manufacturers, merchants, sailors, men of thought, men of action and men of business. I am myself surprised at the large number of adhesions which our protests receive among the intelligent classes of all countries, independently of the labouring masses.

I have heard Lord Avebury speaking and upholding his ideas in Paris, side by side with our illustrious savant M. Berthelot, and I thought that governments were guilty of a great imprudence in allowing such men the honour of denouncing their mistakes.

There is one thing in particular which is shocking. It is not so much the magnitude as the insufficiency of naval and military expenditure that is always affirmed.

Rightly or wrongly, Great Britain is at the head of this schedule of expenditure. One might believe that she had the right to halt, and to declare herself satisfied at least for a time; but no. Lord Roberts declares that never has the British Army been so insufficient as during the period in which it has demanded so many sacrifices. The same striking fact holds good of the Italian Navy and for the majority of other countries. As to France, the battle-ships and guns of the naval programme of 1900, for the execution of which a so-called exceptional and temporary effort of 800,000,000 francs was demanded of us, are declared old-fashioned before their completion. We must recommence and redouble the same effort in 1906. The strength of future battle-ships will be raised to 18,000 tons, and they are being rendered so complicated as to run the risk of rendering them unworkable on the day of battle. The urgency is such that the Minister of Marine does not furnish Parliament with any information, so to speak, concerning the plans decided upon. The amount of the expenditure is spoken of, that is all. A Senator, M. Pichon, demands that at least a trial should be given to the turbine system adopted in other countries; labour is lost, but no one listens; people vote with their eyes shut, so quickly that it is seen three months later—well, before the commencement of the new constructions, that the plans are not yet complete. Thus the programme of 1900 has become old-fashioned before it is finished, that of 1906 being so even before it was voted.

All this is known. Some of our writers and orators do not fail to reproach our Government on this ground instead of attacking them for the inevitable tendencies of militarism, and I have reason to believe, without wishing to offend anyone, that the evil is not worse in France than elsewhere, although we make more noise; perhaps it is even less.

Yet we are in times of Peace! What would the expenses be in case of war? How would the belligerents provide for their own existence? How would they assure the provisions, ammunition and ambulance services for their armies and navies? These are all questions put forward with a prophetic insight by our lamented friend Jean de Bloch. These are all new questions, for to-day we have no longer armies but peoples in presence of each other, questions to which it will be understood no one can reply, but so obscure and disquieting that in the eyes of all reasonable men the risks of war are a thousand times greater than its advantages. Without taking into account the formidable uncertainty of battle, war settles nothing. It is a task that must always commence over again, and yet people prepare for it and ruin themselves in doing so. That is the general opinion. And each war which, in spite of the progress of public opinion, breaks out again through the faults of governments, not only shakes popular confidence in the necessity of a pacific organisation but the authority of governments. The Russo-Japanese war has not discouraged a single man of good faith, and when one hears incorrigible Chauvinism say that Russia prepared her defeat by dreams of The Hague Conference, we all know, alas! that she would have avoided it if she had remained faithful to her pacific programme.

On the other hand, it is obvious that the Japanese would not have gone to war if Europe had not herself led them on. They have made war to recover advantages or guarantees of which war had deprived them. A policy of justice and foresight in the Far East would have prevented the expeditions, conflicts, revolts and conflagrations that had been let loose. The Japanese victories are the consequence of the mistakes of Europe, but the results of those mistakes are not confined to these victories. Let us pass rapidly over the financial consequences of militarism to its social and political consequences. That will be a veritable chastisement, if so many warnings have been repeated to no purpose.

REVOLT.

Public opinion cannot be prevented from seeing in the Russian revolution the most eloquent of object-lessons. Henceforth these two words, war and revolution, are inseparable. War is the preface, in the present case it has been the school of the revolution. People assert that the Russian soldiers who have returned to their homes, without counting the widows, orphans and forsaken mothers, have become so many apostles of revolution, and that thus an inverted mobilisation has been effected with such perfect accuracy that not a single village has escaped from the contagion, since there is not a village that has not had some of its children with the colours. But let us set aside the hypothesis of war, and confine ourselves exclusively to the effects of armed Peace such as it exists. It will suffice to discredit governments if they persist in maintaining it in spite of its unpopularity. An opposition will be formed in all countries against their inaction.

The recent General Elections in England and France have given a crushing majority to the partisans of a limitation of military burdens. Those partisans are everywhere gaining ground. In Germany the number of Socialists and Radicals in the Reichstag has considerably increased. In a general way it may be affirmed that the progress of the most advanced parties in all countries is in proportion to the increase of unproductive expenditure. These parties, whatever may be their name, only see in the system of armed Peace a diversion to prevent peoples from demanding reforms, because, once in agreement, it is evident that the peoples would not fail to regulate their progress according to one another, that is to say, according to the progress of the most favoured people.

Already sufficient diffusion of knowledge and ideas has been effected all over the world to enable everyone to compare the burdens of his own country with those of others, which will put an end to the general excess of those burdens.

Everybody recognises that the limitation of armaments will gradually have as a corollary the reduction of the hours of labour, the reduction of the price of goods, the development of the country, the improvement of transport, of public instruction, of hygiene, and the adoption of social reforms. People calculate what a country might do in the way of constructing railways, bridges, ports, machinery, schools and museums with merely a part of the money which is devoted to naval and military budgets.

People think of the workmen lacking in workshops and for agricultural labour. Everybody also measures the progress made by the countries of the New World and the extent of their privileges.

It is well known from what these privileges are derived, and why, not having our burdens, they produce and sell at the lowest figure. It is in vain that it is attempted to erect Customs barriers. Tariff wars further aggravate the bitterness of economic struggles. Social antagonisms are fomented by international antagonisms. Little by little people are becoming habituated to the idea as to the necessity for a new social order, which is taking form in the popular imagination in contrast to that which now exists, and the question arises whether governments will favour or oppose this evolution; whether they will be the auxiliaries which it is necessary to support, or obstacles that must be overthrown.

It rests with the governments to settle this question in a manner creditable to themselves. For my part I refuse to accept any pessimistic conclusion. The popular masses are not inspired by any preconceived, evil sentiment in any country. If eventually they become exasperated and finish by losing patience, they are, on the other hand, thankful for the slightest progress, from whatever side it may come, and for the least sympathy shown for their interests, provided that this sympathy is sincere, and is not manifested too late. Remember the universal enthusiasm that greeted the creation of the first Hague Conference. It was really the opening of a new era for public opinion.

By whom if not by the republican masses was the King of England received in Paris later, in 1903, and after what a crisis? And what was the significance of that impressive welcome. It was that the people did justice to the courageous work of appeasement which the King had accomplished. It was that the people recognised in that work their own aspirations, and that they were happy to see this dream finally a living reality. Whoever has since then come in the same disposition, sovereign, head of State, or Foreign Minister, has found the same welcome in that capital and throughout all France.

It is not, therefore, by blind resistance that governments will preserve their authority. It is by their intelligence, by their promptitude in understanding popular aspirations. Those among them who recognise this fact will inherit in universal history the places formerly reserved for conquerors, and their country will owe them more than laurels, namely, prosperity.

CONCLUSION.

I have finished. I desire to make my conclusion very modest. I do not demand, no one amongst us demands, disarmament, nor even for the moment the reduction of armaments; but we are certain that the limitation of naval and military expenses is a reasonable act, an act of patriotic foresight for the governments of all countries without exception.

It is in vain for people to raise the objection against me that concerted limitation is difficult and that I have not even indicated on what bases and by what means it could be brought about. What will be the common standard? How are the following considerations to be taken into account, namely, the area of States, the extent and vulnerability of their frontiers and of their coasts, the extent of their population, their economic and financial strength and the importance of their colonies? And if such an agreement were established how could it be enforced?

Let our opponents be reassured. The bases and the means of a general limitation will be found, if the Powers seek them in good faith. But have they tried to find them?

No; this inquiry is yet to be made. Up to the present people have confined themselves to the usual negations, always opposed to so-called dreams of progress. They wait until public opinion forces them to go ahead, and that is why we should address ourselves to public opinion rather than to governments. If we commence with the governments they will say that they are powerless, or they will reverse the rôles. They will ask us to do the work for them and to undertake ourselves the solution which we urge them to find. We will not commit this puerile blunder of proposing, (in the present state of feeling, a system of which it would be only too easy for governments to emphasise the weak points as a means of enabling them to maintain the *status quo*, for there is no system in the world which can take the place of the goodwill of governments.

Systems are not wanting for limiting armaments by common agreement, without imprudence and without injustice. But the essential point, and the most difficult to find, is the goodwill necessary for this limitation to become a reality, and not one more disappointment after so many others. It was possible to come to an understanding at The Hague, on a principle, but that understanding will only be really efficacious on the day when governments understand that their interest is to apply it, the day when every nation shall have discovered that it is weakening instead of strengthening itself by expenditure disproportionate to its resources. This discovery is so simple that it will be realised as if by enchantment, in some years, perhaps in some months, by the public opinion of nations which are now brought closer together. It is our rôle to work so that the delay shall be as short as possible. Let us not allow ourselves to be diverted by idle challenges. Let us not furnish governments with excuses for throwing their own work on our shoulders. Our rôle is to stimulate and not to usurp the functions of governments. Our rôle is to create public opinion, or rather to reveal to all peoples that they have but one and the same opinion, and that governments ought to concert and contrive to obey that opinion.

Is that, then, a barren rôle? I believe it, on the contrary, to be indispensable and decisive. If we succeed in persuading public opinion, all the rest will follow. It will even be a matter of indifference whether a general agreement is arrived at between

governments. A clearly defined desire among
several nations to put an end to their mutual increase of military expenditure will suffice to bring
about a general arrest of that expenditure even
better than an agreement. The sincere goodwill
of some will be more efficacious than the mistrust
of all. An initial current will be established and
its force will be such that no government can dream
of going against it. And even admitting, to assume
the worst, that any government would take the
responsibility for such a retrograde and blind resistance, it would exhaust itself at home and abroad,
without there being any necessity, as our adversaries
contend, to declare war against it. It would destroy
itself.

To speak out plainly, we ought certainly to demand
and obtain the inclusion of the question of limitation
in the programme of the second Hague Conference.
That would officially consecrate its existence, its
actuality, and its gravity. This consecration will be
an encouragement for us all; it will also have the
advantage of awakening public opinion. It will
constitute a sort of declaration of the urgency of the
discussion claimed by us and officially accepted, but
it will not suffice. It is not enough that the question of limitation should be included in the
programme—it must be taken into consideration.
If not, the governments, even those of good faith,
will not emerge from the vicious circle of their
impotence. The question of limitation will not be
solved but eluded, under ridiculous conditions which
will exasperate public opinion.

I speak of it without pessimism, indeed, on the
contrary, as an optimist who has seen things close

at hand, and who refuses to renew experiments
already made and doomed in advance to failure.
We should not forget that already, in 1899, the
question was included in the programme of the
Conference, and was even placed at the head of
that programme, without any other result than its
summary adjournment.   Why?   Let us frankly
recognise it, because public opinion was still in
complete ignorance, because our protest had not
been organised, because the question of limitation
was too new, too unknown, and had not been the
object of any consideration.   Distinguished people
in several countries had studied the means of legally
settling international conflicts.   The question of
Arbitration had for a long time deeply engaged the
best minds.   Memorable experiments, which had
proved eminently fortunate and fruitful, had been
made in this direction by governments themselves,
beginning with that of Mr. Gladstone.   It is impossible to ignore such precedents as the *Alabama*
affair, and the treaty between Italy and the
Argentine Republic.   But what a difference in the
case of the limitation of armaments!   No one, not
a single government, not a single one of their
representatives—not even the most devoted—had ever
ventured to seek for a solution to the problem.   This
problem, although of universal interest, was over-
looked by thinking people all over the world.   Poli-
ticians regarded it as insoluble and men of science
as a matter of indifference—since its solution
depended upon the caprice of governments or upon
their combinations—consequently it could only cease
to be insoluble when it ceased to be a matter of
indifference.   On the other hand, the evil of armed

Peace was still accepted, even with its excesses, as an evil necessary for the maintenance of the Peace of the world. It was so rigorously imposed by patriotic discipline in each State that the search for a remedy could not fail to have the appearance of weakness or imprudence. Protests were rare and of slight importance. People complained more than they protested.

In reality the study of the question of limitation was not open; it was subordinated to the education of public opinion and the progress of general pacification. It could only come in its turn after Arbitration had taken root.

That was why the Conference of 1899 altered the plan of its labours. In order to avoid a scandalous breakdown in confining its activity to the postponement of the limitation of armaments and certain small matters, as also to respond to generous and wise aspirations, it undertook the problem of a permanent international jurisdiction. It created the Tribunal of The Hague. This considerable result cost three months of almost daily difficult and passionate discussions. It was necessary to overcome obstinate resistance and to moderate thoughtless demands. It was necessary to reduce to its real proportions the famous question of penalty, which had been greatly exaggerated. That penalty, of which we had always been accused of losing sight, was, of course, lacking on that occasion, as it still is to the new international jurisdiction. This lacuna was then as now brought forward as an objection to our scheme. Nevertheless, The Hague Tribunal has asserted itself without having called in any *gendarmerie* to secure the execution of its awards. We are satisfied with the force of public opinion and the moral authority which it places at the service of justice. Have we been deceived? Who will pretend that in the eyes of the world a government could with impunity refuse to submit to the judgment of the tribunal which had condemned it and reject its competence after having accepted it? In the same way a government which should try to check the limitation of armaments, or should violate the rules of that limitation after having consented thereto, would incur a formidable reproach. It would place itself in a false position and group against it too many adverse elements.

Moral penalties for the enforcement of the limitation of armaments, like those for Arbitration, will be more efficacious than material penalties, even if they could be found. They exist* in the

---

* It is really unreasonable to count public opinion as nothing and the law as everything when one constantly sees public opinion make, abolish, and recast laws. Under the pretext that laws are not always obeyed, and that they are still less eternal, are we to renounce the making of laws? No. Let us admit, therefore, that there are ephemeral laws and effective verdicts of public opinion, and let us not consider the penalties imposed by the latter as negligible.

Besides, the question of the insufficiency of penalties which is brought forward as an objection, by the so-called right-minded, against our efforts to organise international justice to limit armaments, is nothing else but an argument for gaining time like all the others. The truth is that to secure the approval of the right-minded, to which I refer, one ought to change nothing and to improve nothing. One of the best of them, M. Charles Benoist, for whom I have a certain weakness because he is an exception to the rule, and who never misses an opportunity of exercising all his wit at the expense of my generous chimeras, when he speaks of the penalty imposed by public opinion, which his

consciences of peoples, to-day enlightened neighbours. Their power is daily growing. Let us not
wait to find something better. Let us devote ourselves exclusively to throwing full light on the
question before the new Hague Conference. Let us
be on our guard. This Conference, if it fails, might
partially destroy the hopes to which the first had
given birth. Certain of our adversaries already
discount the ground we might lose by the failure of
our manifestation. They amuse themselves with
the idea of the clever trick which the governments
might play the Conference in entrusting it with a
premature and impossible task. To convoke a
Conference of The Hague in order that it should
discredit itself; to render it responsible for a failure
which it could not avoid—what an unhoped-for
result! What a double coup that would be to leave
to the Conference the task of burying the project
of limitation.

---

friends forbid me to adduce in favour of my theory, expressed
himself as follows, in 1894, in his book "La Politique," pp.
54 & 55 :—

"Public opinion is organised from the present time (1894) and
will be more and more endowed with an actual power, the extent
of which it would be impossible to exaggerate. Of itself alone
it has produced, in the political world, a revolution comparable to
those produced in the economic world by the application of steam
and electricity."

In the same work M. Charles Benoist invokes this opinion of
Sumner Maine apropos of the *coup d'état*.

Does a *coup d'état* become legal when it succeeds ? Yes, should
say the advocates of penalty, but, No, responds M. Charles Benoist.
What is the real penalty which he opposes to the pretended
legality ? The disapprobation of the people, the disgrace inflicted
by public opinion (Ibid, p. 55.)

It is nevertheless this double fiasco which awaits us if we are foolish enough to go to The Hague a second time without previous study, without consideration, and without preliminary preparation. This time the Conference will no longer have the same resource as in 1899 of devoting its labours to another item of its programme. All the other items will be insignificant compared with the limitation of armaments, for which the whole world is waiting. It will be condemned to avow its impotence and declare its own bankruptcy.

If we have not sufficient time to prepare public opinion between now and next year it would be better to postpone the meeting of the Conference to 1908 rather than convoke it at the risk of its destruction. Let us in any event hasten to bring about an inquiry, and to organise the agitation which should precede the consideration of such a serious matter. Let us not admit that this deliberation can be improvised. Let us appeal to the conscience and to the reason of even those who had previously considered it to be their patriotic duty, or even a necessity, to pay no attention to the matter. Let each of us appeal to his own constituents, to those who have entrusted us with their representation, and have given us their confidence; let us appeal likewise in our own countries to the press, and show it what an honest, sterling popularity it could acquire for itself in supporting us; and, finally, let us appeal to our various parliaments, each to the parliament of which he is a member. In a word, I return to the preoccupation by which I was inspired at the commencement of this report, namely, that all international action should be supported by national preparation. Let each of us increase his efforts in order that the question of limitation should become ripe, and familiar to a large proportion of the élite of the enlightened public, before being handed over to the diplomatists. Let each State commence by studying the question for itself, if it really intends to undertake its solution with the other States. That of itself will be an indication. Let The Hague Conference be placed in possession of a certain number of complete projects. Let it have an *embarras du choix* between French, English, American, German, Italian and other projects. Let it have, so to speak, as many projects as there are countries, so that its only task will be to reconcile them. While an agreement of different international projects will be possible, a conflict between the ignorance of the different nationalities would be certain.

I repeat that the question is urgent. Public patience is being exhausted. The public feel that a conclusion could be arrived at, if desired. It will be grateful to those who act as its interpreters and protest in its name. Let us not wait for it to revolt. I consider it a privilege for the French Parliamentary Group for the Promotion of Arbitration that its President has had the honour of formulating this protest.

D'ESTOURNELLES DE CONSTANT,

Member of The Hague Tribunal,
Member of the French Senate.

INTERPARLIAMENTARY UNION

LIMITATION

OF

Naval and Military Expenditure

Report drawn up in the Name of the Commission entrusted with
the discussion of this problem at the Conference of the Union in Rome
in the Month of October 1911

BY

M. D'ESTOURNELLES DE CONSTANT

Member of the French Senate

*The Report is preceded by a preface recalling
the circumstances that prevented the meeting of the Conference in Rome*

1912

MISCH & THRON

PUBLISHERS
BRUSSELS
Rue Royale, 126

PRÉFACE

The most opportune of epidemics having broken out to prevent the meeting of the Interparliamentary Conference at Rome, it has not been possible to discuss the report which follows before the Conference. The question was raised as to whether it would not be proper to publish it. The Bureau of the Union decided the question in the affirmative, and such was also the opinion of all the members of the Commission who, partaking of the same patriotic sentiments, joined in the drawing up of the report and affixed their signature to it.

This report is the result of great labour and serious consideration. The time is all the better chosen to publish it that the increase of armaments is more than ever to the fore. We willingly stand up, each in his own country, against the ironical or indignant protests, and closely unite together, we, Members of Parliament of four great military Powers, Germany, Great Britain, France and Russia, in the expression of our common belief that the limitation of armaments imposes itself to all. Ruin, revolution and anarchy become more and more the only and certain consequences of the competition for armed peace. We foresee the numerous conflicts which threaten to obscure the horizon of civilisation, but everyone also perceives, in the dazzling light of the experience of the last few years, that these conflicts may be solved amicably either by the efforts of Diplomacy, now more necessary than ever, or by organised practical Arbitration.

It is true that the Turco-Italian war appears to have given a brutal denial to our hopes or belief ; we deplore that it should have been begun in defiance of the solemn engagements contracted by the belligerent parties at the Hague. We did not fail, within the limits of our power, to insist that amicable mediation should endeavour to put an end to the war, the possible complications of which are a danger to all the world. But, having declared this, we cannot admit that the events which have troubled Europe for the last six months lessen the force of the conclusions of our report. A Turkish fleet, whatever may have been said, would have been but a useless thing and a further complication; it would not have prevented the surprise of the landing at Tripoli, which the Turkish army, under exceptionally favourable circumstances, permitted without resistance. The legitimate claims of Italy would certainly have been done justice to, peaceably, before a Congress, as it happened for France in 1878 concerning Tunis at the Berlin Congress.

As to the difficulties which have arisen between France, Germany, Spain and Great Britain concerning Morocco, these prove that the Governments involved were intent on remaining peaceful, since a war was not brought about, while in former times it would have been considered unavoidable; this also proves that, despite the most threatening complications, public opinion, better educated than in the past, weighed so heavily in favour of peace that the complications were smoothed over, and an agreement took the place of disorder. Opinion gradually educates itself; it begins to understand the realities of international life, that we can avoid war, but not the incidents and conflicts which accompany all organisations, whether social, national or international. We have the power to prevent or to bring about war, but we cannot prevent difficulties from arising. We must therefore be prepared to see them arise more numerous as nations hold closer intercourse with each other, and they will then no longer surprise us. We shall consider them as more or less natural obstacles which Peace alone can really solve in honourable and lasting fashion.

If such be the case, why persist in preparing useless war against one another? Why not apply the strength and wealth which we are wasting to fertile work, which to-day solicits the activity and co-operation of all civilised nations?

Only a part of the world is put to use; why then fight over the remainder which is so much beyond our present expansive possibilities? Why not come to an understanding, by mutual arrangement, to no longer work unproductively, but to create and progress.

Why not open to science, to the ardent and ambitious youth of all countries, new fields of battle, glorious ones where the most generous emulation is found, and where pride without hatred or retaliation rises solely against nature.

When the twentieth century will have thrown aside Machiavellian tradition it may realise a magnificent dream for the benefit of each and the glory of all.

The thought that, despite all, we are approaching the dawn of a new era, and that an economic co-operation scheme may be entered into by all the signatory powers of the Hague Convention to take the place bygone antagonism, this thought gives more force to the i 1 which has urged us on in our thankless but good fight f conciliation, international justice and the limitation of armaments.

Interparliamentary Union

LIMITATION OF NAVAL AND MILITARY EXPENDITURE

REPORT OF THE COMMISSION (1) AND DRAFT RESOLUTION
APPROVED BY THE COUNCIL AT ITS SITTING, APRIL 8TH 1911

INTRODUCTION

Patriotic Limitation

It is as a patriot, in the interests of my country as in the interests of each civilised country, that I have consented to return to the question of the limitation of armaments. It is humiliating to begin the report with which my colleagues have, as in 1906, entrusted me, by such a declaration, but we address ourselves not only to those who know us, but also to those whose opinion is biassed or misinformed. We must not tire to make ourselves clear on this point.

None of us would give up his firm intention to defend his country with all his power; not only the mother country, but Liberty, Right and Justice. The existence of the mother country, the independence and security of each nation are the essential conditions of good international relations; without nations there would be no internationalism. Peace is only the security of a nation guaranteed by all the other nations; without this security Peace would be empty of meaning, it would be merely a threat in disguise.

---

(1) This Commission is composed of Mr. d'Estournelles de Constant (France), Chairman, Herr Conrad Haussmann (Germany), M. Paul Milioukov (Russia) and the Rt. Hon. Lord Weardale (Great Britain).

This is armed Peace. Armed Peace is no more a solution than war. We have proclaimed this over and over again.

If as Patriots we wish to study the means of limiting the naval and military burdens which crush the greatest civilised nations, it is by convincing ourselves that the increase of this unproductive expenditure is a weakening, not a strengthening factor for each country, an imprudent, not a precautionary measure. We must not admit that, under cover of a protection which ever grows heavier, the native country which we love, be weakened and given up to the hazards, the surprises, the revolts which cannot fail to arise from the universal lassitude.

We do not dwell in a fool's paradise; we know that since 1906, when our last resolution was voted by acclamation at the London Conference, the question has not advanced one step; but the resistance which we have met with, and also the attacks which have been made upon us have not discouraged us, they have stimulated us, and they show how deep is the sore we are trying to heal.

For the most part Governments have attempted nothing towards the realisation of our resolution, of their own resolution, because it was in 1899 and 1907, at the two Hague Conferences, that the question of the limitation of armaments, brought up by the Emperor of Russia, was, with the unanimous assent of the Powers represented, placed on the order paper to be solved or at least studied. Force of inertia has responded to these appeals.

Force of inertia is neither a remedy nor an argument; it is not almighty; another power, an irresistible one, the natural course of things will tread it down. Progress, the levelling power of knowledge and information will prove to evidence that war is no longer a solution, as it must ever be renewed. War gives birth to revenge and indefinite bickerings. Again, war has become so ruinous, so complicated, so destructive to many bountiful activities, throwing into the field millions of men, sacrificing milliards, and would be such a fearful lottery for all, that not a single reasonable or responsible being would risk letting the monster loose. Then, if simple common sense is awakened, if all civilised states recognise that war is no longer a resource, a. if all nations are happy to see Conciliation and Arbitration ta. the place of violence, by what unaccountable contradiction w ! each state continue its race to ruin in order to prepare war, detested and condemned by all?

This contradiction is self-evident; it has achieved more than all the anarchistic doctrines to discredit governmental authority and give nations an example of incoherence.

We are all agreed without distinction of party or country, each in the national interests of his country and in the superior interests of all, to ask the 17th Interparliamentary Conference to expressly renew this year our protest of 1906 and to insist that our wish, thanks to interparliamentary action, be at last considered by Governments. Parliamentary authority is now at stake, and public opinion would never forgive its representatives for disinteresting themselves from such a question.

We do not overstep the limits of our mandate; we do not presume to offer governments a ready made solution, for we have too long studied the problem of limitation not to be aware of its complexity. It is brought before each country with its distinct natural elements : the navy is to the fore in one country, whereas in another the army is first, or again the navy and army rival each other in activity. Perhaps aerial or submarine navigation have progressed in one country more than elsewhere, but everywhere wireless telegraphy, the use of explosives or mines have completely transformed the art of war. A country may be protected against aggression by the nature of its soil, or its seaboard, or by distance, better than another with dangerous surroundings. A small country may better assure its security with proportionally smaller means than its more populated neighbours. Limitation is a question of species, a geographical question, a national question of the first importance; such a question can only be usefully and reasonably studied by the country itself, but all countries having an equal interest in its solution, it becomes an international problem. It does not suffice to call upon each country to limit its armaments. The rivalry which ruins them all must cease.

We would say to each country : remain armed for your defence, keep your armaments up to the standard which you think useful, but agree between yourselves to reduce this measure instead of increasing it. Once you have entered into this path, you will discover that a minimum of armaments gives more security, with less expense, than a maximum. What we ask is for a change in the point of view; instead of blindly increasing naval and military expenditure, make a point of reducing them each of you and in your interest. Let us suppose, to take into account the ever-ready argument of sceptics, that a single state refuse to enter into these views and remain obstinate, even supposing that this State believe itself to be master of the world by reason of its being the only one to have preserved its maximum strength, it would in reality have the whole world against it, not only from sentiment, — and sentiment is not to be neglected — but from pure solidarity, because it would be the only obstacle to the progress of all.

Its situation would soon become unbearable both internally and externally, from an international as well as from a social point of view. The interests of the most powerful nations is to reduce their armaments and that immediately. If ten years more are allowed to pass it will be too late. Revolution will be begotten of armed peace. It is high time to look into the question, if governments do not wish the matter to be solved without their aid, despite them and against them, « ab absurdo », by excess of harm.

Already we notice the immense gap created between the continual progress of educated opinion and the stolidness of governments. Governments are like industries, they must be prepared for perpetual transformation. They must give themselves the pains and time to think. The problems which they solved, or which yesterday they found already solved, are no longer the same to-day and they will be different to-morrow. They must be thought over indefinitely. It is too easy not to change when everything changes around us and to remain attached to traditional truth. An eminent and highly educated General, but nearing the sixties, said to me two years ago with uncommon sincerity : « I do not wish to believe in aviation, it would upset all I have learnt; I cannot begin life over again ». Public opinion has the benefit over modest generals and admirals to have nothing to unlearn. It educates itself from day to day by the sight of progress which appears at all points of the globe. But the representatives of public opinion must be instructed, so that in their turn they may instruct governments. Then the point of view of governments will change, and instead of throwing disorder into the State's finance in order to keep up the rivalry of barren expense with their neighbours, they will understand that their interest lies in their agreeing together to restore order for the good of each.

We have said, and we repeat it, that the campaign we pursue is in view of restoring order, in fact a purely patriotic campaign.

In order not to refer our colleagues to too numerous works which have already appeared, and also to furnish them with a digest of the arguments which have for years past formed and fortified our belief, we have thought useful to accompany our wish by the following statement.

STATEMENT.

The Council of the Interparliamentary Union resolved last year at Brussels, on the 1ˢᵗ of September 1910, to confide to a special Commission the drawing up of a new resolution in favour of the limitation of naval and military expenditure.

This Commission, composed of Herr Conrad Haussmann, Member of the Reichstag, for Germany, Mr. Milioukov, Member of the Duma, for Russia, Lord Weardale, for Great Britain, Mr. d'Estournelles de Constant, for France, Mr. Chr. L. Lange, General Secretary of the Union, met in Paris under the presidency of Mr. d'Estournelles de Constant and adopted the following text and the considerations which precede; the Council of the Union decided, at its sitting of April 8th last at Brussels, that the resolution should form part of the program of the 17th Conference, which is to take place at Rome on October 3rd next.

The following are the principal motives which have determined your Commission to propose to you to adopt this resolution.

Governmental and Conservative Origin of the Projects of Limitation.

No one could without being prejudiced consider as subversive or superficial a resolution which merely reproduces the opinions expressed by the two Hague Conferences, and which were themselves but the attenuated reproductions of the official proposition of the Russian Government as expressed in the memorable Mouravieff Circular of August 24th 1908, and couched in terms which cannot be too often called to mind.

Count Mouravieff, Minister for Foreign Affairs, to the Representatives of the Powers accredited at St. Petersburg.

St. Petersburg, 12/24 August 1908.

The maintenance of universal Peace and a possible reduction of the excessive armaments which weigh on all nations present themselves as the Ideal to which the efforts of all Governments should tend.

Convinced that this high aim responds to the most essential interests and legitimate wishes of all Powers, the Imperial Government esteems that the present moment would be most favourable to the investigation, by means of international discussion, as to the most effectual means of assuring to all nations the bounties of a real and durable peace and above all of putting an end to the progressive development of present armaments.

During the last twenty years the yearning for a general pacification has affirmed itself in the conscience of civilised nations.

The preservation of peace has been put forward as the aim of international politics; to follow this path great States have entered into powerful alliances.

It is to guarantee Peace that they have developed their military forces to proportions which were up till now unheard of, and which they continue to increase, undeterred by any sacrifice.

Notwithstanding all these efforts the beneficent results of Peace have not yet been attained.

The financial burdens in continual progress strike public prosperity *at its root;* the intellectual and physical strength of nations, capital and labour, are for the most part diverted from their natural application and *consumed unproductively.* Hundreds of millions are employed to acquire *fearful engines of destruction, which, considered to-day as the most perfect that science can produce, are doomed to lose to-morrow all their worth by reason of some new discovery of science in this field.* National culture, the progress of economy, the production of wealth are paralysed, or turned aside from their true path.

The increase of armaments of each Power draw Governments further and further from the proposed goal. The economic difficulties and the continual danger which lies in the pile of war material, transforms the armed peace of our time into a crushing burden which nations carry with greater and greater difficulty.

It is evident that should this situation continue, it would lead to the catastrophe which it is supposed to avoid, and the horrors of which cause human thought to shudder.

To put an end to these incessant armaments and to find the means of preventing the calamities which threaten the whole world, such is the suprême duty which is imposed to-day on all nations.

Inspired by this sentiment H. M. the Emperor has been pleased to command me to propose to all Governments with accredited Representatives at the Imperial Court to convene a Conference to study this important problem.

Count MOURAVIEFF.

No one can pretend, though it has been said, that this eloquent appeal was uselesss, since it was followed by the two Hague Conferences; but regarding the limitation of armaments it has only produced the two following motions :

Opinion pressed in 1899 :

On the pr. position of M. Léon Bourgeois :

« The Conference esteems that the progressive limitation of armaments which actually weigh upon the world is highly desirable for the moral and material good of humanity. »

Opinion expressed in 1907 :

The Conference unanimously adopted the following resolution.

« The second Peace Conference confirms the resolution adopted by the 1899 Conference in regard to the limitation of naval and military expenditure and, considering that this expenditure has considerably increased since the said year, the Conference declares that it would be highly desirable to see Governments resume this question for serious consideration. »

The proposition of Russia and the wishes expressed by the two Hague Conferences were not put aside by all Governments. Propositions were made by the British Government. No one has forgotten the speech delivered on March 9th 1899 in the English Parliament by Mr. Goschen, Conservative Member of the Cabinet, the categorical and confirmative letter of Mr. Joseph Chamberlain, Member of the Conservative Cabinet, in July 1903 and the repeated declarations of Sir Henry Campbell-Bannerman, Liberal Prime Minister, etc.; nor the declarations of President Roosevelt in the United States. But all these demonstrations have, as is well known, been discouraged and finally put aside.

But should this be a reason for us to be discouraged? No! These propositions have been put aside, it is true, but without any enthusiasm and, as we might say, by slight of hand, each one proclaiming audibly before the public opinion of his country that he would be willing to take the matter into consideration, but could not initiate the movement, or that he was compelled to regulate his actions on those of his strongest armed neighbour; excuses being given by either side, either making a lie of the proverb that a door must be opened or shut; if none would open the door to limitation, none dared to close it. This suspense is still encouraging, it is progress; it has come from our parliamentary action, so coldly received, but which has kept it alive. This report would be incomplete if we omitted to mention the action which takes place more and more frequently everywhere in favour of the idea. Even in France, where the patriotic feeling is made keener by painful remembrance, we have heard frequent debates in 1910 and 1911 on this question in Parliament, without consequence at first, but at last followed by a favourable resolution. An account of these debates was published by the Interparliamentary Union in its precious *Documents*, which will soon become the official archives of a cause, non existant ten years ago, but which will soon contribute to the diffusion of the arguments of our Commission. The orators taking part in these debates, apart from MM. Jaurès and

Sembat of the Socialist party, to which I have not desired to yield the monopoly of these discussions, were MM. Paul Meunier Charles Dumont, reporter of the Budget, etc., to mention only the Chamber of Deputies. But as early as 1906 this question was closely examined by the actual Secretary for War M. Messimy, then reporter on the Budget, who in the interests of national defence, advocated limitation; this was in 1906 at the London Conference. M. Messimy's paper appears in the Report of the Conference of 1906.

In the United States MM. Burton, Bartholdt, Tawney and others have fought the good battle before Congress. In Italy and Austria the Deputies Bissolati and Seitz have proposed a limitation suitable to their respective countries.

In England the ranks of the partisans of limitation grow every day, appealing to the Liberal Cabinet to remain true to the spirit of Gladstone and Campbell-Bannerman. We find in the Commons our colleagues G. N. Barnes, Thomas Lough, Henry Twist, Robert Harcourt, Ogden, Philip Snowden, Murray Macdonald, G. H. Dickinson, Ponsonby, etc., who sustained for three days, from March 14th to 17th, the debate in 1910.

During the spring of 1911, on the 13th of March, MM. Keir Hardie and King called upon the Secretary for Foreign Affairs to take a standing in the question. In a memorable and sensational speech Sir Edw. Grey did not fear to say, in terms which created a strong impression on public opinion, not only in England, but all over the world, that « *there is a greater danger than that of war, the danger which I once outside this House called bleeding to death in time of Peace* »; adding « the mutual reduction of expenditure, such is the phrase I have always endeavoured to use ».

This question has even been discussed in the German Parliament at the request of several parties. The Interparliamentary Union has published in the above mentioned publications the speeches of our colleagues Eickhoff, Dr Spahn, Haussmann (Wurtemberg) and Prince Schoenaich-Carolath, in response to the discouraging words of the Imperial Chancellor.

All the symptoms have not been decisive, far from it, but all the official declarations were not equally discouraging. Nothing has been done, it is true, but we shall not waste our time in protests, we shall not go out of our way to find out where nor whose is the fault, we must take into account the surroundings, the institutions, the traditions. We all understand this, and it is natural that the French Foreign Minister for example has conformed his speech to that of the German Foreign Minister. We are far from the solution of the problem but it must be clearly put before it can be solved. It is unquestionable that the problems of limitation, disdainfully put aside ten years ago, have risen up and imposed themselves upon us. Here is progress, which, under the pressure of public opinion, will develop rapidly. We must therefore supply public opinion with the needful arguments to uphold its representatives.

The Possibility of realising Limitation.

It would be dangerous to mislead public opinion by presenting the problem of limitation as impossible to solve, when it has been solved under the most difficult and conclusive conditions between the United States of North America and Great Britain. Public opinion will not be long in finding out the truth. It would be difficult to find two nations more violently in conflict than were these two States. The treaty of Dec. 1814, ratified on Feb. 17, 1815, and freely completed by other arrangements among which that of April, 28, 1817, should be thought the most empty of dreams. It put an end to two wars including that of the American Independence; it was even followed by serious hostilities, to name only the battle of New Orleans, memorable to both parties. It left side by side two countries artificially divided on the map, but not effectually on the ground, the United States and Canada, communicating together along a frontier of over 3,000 miles, protected on either side by more than a hundred forts, large and small, by regiments in arms, and by fleets on the big lakes. The names of these forts, Fort Porter, Fort Erie, Fort George, Fort Niagara, etc., call to mind as many fearfully contested battles. And yet it was decided that the two neighbours should disarm, that the fortifications should disappear, and that the guns which armed them should serve to ornament the parks and walks. Could any more precarious situation be conceived than that of these two enemies, one the vanquished master, whose strength had not diminished after Waterloo, and the other the freed State, enfeebled and thinly populated, victorious with the momentary help of the hereditary foe of Great Britain. What rancour, what germs of hatred should have brought to nought a treaty of disarmament leaving these two nations at each other's mercy? I have personally visited this disarmed frontier and have seen the old guns which have become emblems of penitence. No one thinks of violating the treaty, whose hundredth anniversary will be celebrated in three years.

Patriotic and popular rejoicings are being organised for this celebration by our American friends under the Presidency of our indefatigable colleague Mr Burton. Every one will understand that the situation of the old European States is not to be compared to that of the United States and Canada, but it is none the less remarkable that these neighbours have lived in peace for close upon a century in a state of complete and absolute disarmament.

It is also an astonishing fact that up to the time of the internal revolution which has just broken out, Mexico has lived under the same system, next to its powerful neighbour. The reconciliation of Chili and the Argentine Republic is one of the most impressive features which can be mentioned, and is worthy of being better known. But History says little of reconcilement; battles are its chief delight. Our devoted colleague Mr Bartholdt has taken upon himself to fill up, before Congress at Washington, the gap left by History. At the sitting of March 25th 1910 he very ably and eloquently brought to light the treaty of April 1817 which specially relates to naval forces on the big lakes. He read the text which is reproduced in the *Documents* of the Union, n° 3, and known as the Rush-Bagot Treaty (1).

Armaments have increased since 1898. — Naval Expenses. Heavy Tonnages.

The fears of the Russian Government have lost nothing of their appropriateness; on the contrary they are as opportune now as at the time they were uttered. They were but too serious in 1898, when it was high time to put a stop to the excess of military expenditure.

In this sphere powerful nations have not been content with outbidding each other, but have spread contagion far and near. This has determined Governments who had no fleets or no desire to possess any, to acquire them, and we see nations bring their diplomatic influence to bear, in order to further the development not only of interior armaments, but also of the exportation of armaments to foreign lands.

South American Republics have undergone this influence, and several possess fleets of war. Second-hand fleets are even sold

---

(1) See also *Treaties and Conventions concluded between the United States of America and other Powers*, Washington, Government Printing Office, 1871, p. 348. — An interesting study of this treaty was published in the *Revue générale de Droit international public*, September-October 1911, p. 583.

to States loaded with debt, who in order to obtain means or delays are obliged to buy them. What is no longer good for one is deemed good for another. The most astonishing thing is that these facts are supposed to pass unperceived; they are highly demoralising. The force of an explosive is calculated with precision, but no account is taken of the force of public opinion.

We could cite a great number of statistics, but we will take the most impartial, those of M. Théry. He has calculated that the expense of armed peace for Europe alone, leaving aside foreign countries, which are in themselves sufficiently important, has increased from 4,000 millions of francs in 1883 to nearly 8,000 millions in 1908, that is to say a total of 150,000 millions of francs for Europe alone in the space of 25 years. 150,000 millions of francs! Imagine what this would represent in schools, museums, tunnels or canals, in the exploration and development of colonies, in short, in useful work! Can such a waste of resources and energy be imagined, all through lack of agreement and organisation. Happily to-day these statistics are present to all minds, and they show the disproportion between the improductive expenses, ever increasing, and the productive ones more and more reduced.

Here again Governments strangely deceive themselves; their adversaries tell them they are famishing education, universities, laboratories; that highways, hydrographical studies, navigation, commerce, canals, ports and public health are sacrificed to feed the fleets and bring them up to monstrous tonnages, deplored by competent admirals, to mention only the renowned author, Admiral Mahan. Ports are becoming too small and too shallow for the ships, the docks, tools and ammunition will soon fail these monsters, and life will be brought to famine to nurse an idle fancy.

On which side are the day-dreamers? Among the patriots who ask that their country may be opened up and made productive, safely protected, or among those who crush it under the useless armaments of the middle ages?

What will Governments answer when the warships of yesterday, useless, and good only as targets, will encumber their arsenals and they are compelled to sink them to get rid of them, or to preserve them— in what museums?— as proofs of the most costly folly of our age? Their only excuse will be that if they cost so many thousands of millions to Humanity, which was deprived of so much progress, they at least were of no use. It will be objected that not only were they of no use, but some critics will say that if certain States had resisted the temptation to buy fleets and form navies, they would have avoided war, revolution and other irretrievable disasters.

The bid for naval expenses will not even have changed the proportion of the respective forces of the different States,since, when one builds a ship, the other immediately builds two and so on. It will not have given a country the best defensive or offensive weapon as, before a warship is completed, it is already out of date by reason of the progress shown in the last one ordered. Let not people try once more to distort our words under pretence that we attack excesses which we consider disastrous. None of us has ever thought of casting a slur on either the army or the navy of his country; what we all desire is that the army and navy be proportioned to what it should defend, and not crush the country under its weight. We ask the different Parliaments to not blindly accept naval and military estimates when other ones are closely examined and picked to pieces. We desire that these estimates be discussed and voted with a full knowledge of their necessity. Many sailors think, and we cannot sufficiently repeat it, that large tonnages make the navy heavy and impede its natural life, which is to sail and show itself. It is an armour which holds it down, when it should have wings to allow it to spread itself over the world.

Where will this end?

Note the embarrassment of Governments before this simple question. When, ten years ago, we were asked for thousands of millions, we were told, in order evidently to quiet our conscience, that the fleets we were called upon to approve were the final ones — ironclads of 14,500 tons. — Since then it has been shown that they were worthless, and that larger ones were required. This brought us to 18,000 tons from which we easily passed to 20,000 tons, without giving a thought to the cost of building, near 100 millions, and untold extra expenses, which we dare not total up.

The cost, in time of peace, for coal and ammunition — this latter having to be frequently renewed to avoid disasters such as those of the *Iena* and *Maine* — the cost of maintenance of these monsters is so high that they navigate as little as possible in order not to be worn out and impoverish the Exchequer; the exaggeration of tonnage has been the death-blow to navigation, and the navy, admirable means of education and development of human energy, is the first victim of the excess of naval expenditure. If it still be true that victory belongs to the fleets or armies which are used to manœuvre, what will then be the fate of the heavy battleships?

It is true nevertheless that to-day the so-called final tonnage

— 21,000 tons — is outstripped; 25,000 tons is now advocated, and 30,000 tons are foreshadowed in the near future. And when these marvels of naval construction will be afloat, an accident in time of peace, in time of war a torpedo, a bolt from Heaven or from the deep, will suffice to reduce to nought in a few seconds this ship and its thousand or more young men full of life and activity. One need not be a Humanitarian, it is sufficient to be a human being, to rise against such disorder of reason, and it is easy to foresee a general protest so powerful that it must be taken into account, but the error will have been dearly bought and progress greatly impeded.

The Increase of Armaments is not only ineffectual, but disastrous to a Nation; it creates social Convulsions and Strikes.

If it be true that several great nations must invest about two thirds of their income for the preparation of war, one third only of their vitality is left. Two thirds of the taxes paid are unproductive, and one third devoted to the upkeep of national organisation. The burden cast on labour is therefore three times heavier than it should be. Labour must then produce three times more than is necessary, or the results will be reduced by two thirds. This places the heavier armed nations in a state of great inferiority, and they must necessarily become the poorest, the less content and most insecure. The expenses necessary to progress are postponed and salaries cannot be raised in proportion to general circulation and the ever increasing cost of living.

The necessities of the world increase, but sacrifices do not go towards these acquirements; increased squanderings respond to crying necessities. This cannot last indefinitely. Hence strikes, workmen's strikes and public employees' strikes, strikes of all sorts of wage-earners who are not sufficiently paid; hence economic crises and other ills which threaten the peace of the world more than the dangers which armaments are supposed to ward off. The excess of armaments is described to us as a good investment, an insurance, but this is a gross mistake. We create thereby a danger which prevents us from facing the real dangers of our time, dangers which are already sufficiently serious.

The Excess of Armaments is in Contradiction with the Progress of Arbitration.

The only final assurance against war is the diffusion of general education, the institution of international justice, the practice of conciliation, the organization of peace.

War may have appeared formerly as the last argument, the *Ultima ratio Regum*, when recourse to public opinion was inexistant and heads of States could say « I am the State ». But to-day general sentiment is not alone against war, it is common interest, national interest, professional and individual interest, in fact all human interests which rise against a few private individuals.

This is a complete change, a definite change, resulting from general intercourse. Nations can no longer be led astray as was the case when they lived in ignorance and isolation; now they know one another, they converse, whereas formerly each was a bug-bear to the other. Nations have now understood that they must have an organisation, similar to that of individuals, to create a judiciary power, which however imperfect, will always be better than the hazardous game of blows. Thus Arbitration has been instituted between States, just as Courts of Justice among individuals, and the first results of this institution have been so conclusive that they have imposed themselves to the confidence and attention of all.

Public opinion does not admit that this progr s of arbitration be ignored or laughed at. To laugh at arbitrati n to-day would be to openly throw scorn at nations. Formerly public opinion trembled when Governments spoke of war; now it becomes impatient at the thought, knowing that Conciliation and Arbitration are at its disposal, and this impatience is to be feared. It will no longer allow Governments to play with fire, but considers that their duty is to avoid conflagration, not to produce it.

National Defence and Limitation.

Only senseless beings — and whatever may be said they are rather rare — would make light of the fate of their country; as good citizens profit by modern progress in order to develop their activity, as their independence and dignity grow, the more their sense of duty towards national defence develops; in the same way a father would defend his child, his family, his home. But as man has given up defending himself alone and placed himself, whether he will or no, under the protection of national justice, he would like to know, international justice being to day existant, whether he could not place himself under its laws. Such is the chain of deductions which none can prevent independent and sincere thought from following, and the fact that Governments have refused to accept this chain of thought as natural, appears to all impartial men as an inconceivable phenomenon.

The Government that would réduce spontaneously its naval and military armaments within possible limits would be exposed to fewer dangers than the one who impoverishes the country by imposing excessive sacrifice upon it. In case of aggression the one would have fewer battleships, but more enthusiasm among its indignant population, more resource and more sympathies and more support from universal opinion. The Transvaal war has shown what defence can be made by an unarmed people. What would then be that of a really national army having received a preparatory education at school, and which was trained, not overworked.

State of Inferiority of great military Nations in economic Struggles.

Great show is made of the prosperity of great military nations, but the dark side is hidden from view. Little is said of the difficulties and competitions to be overcome under unequal conditions. The winners are not always the most wealthy nor the strongest.

They are enticed and led astray by victory. To some defeat has been a terrible lesson, but their prosperity dates precisely from their military defeat. The defeat of Iena served the growth of Prussia. A more recent example is that of Denmark. Apparently doomed fifty years age, Denmark has literally transformed itself; it has thrown aside its ancient traditions; from a wheat-growing country it has become a cattle-breading centre. Education, the spirit of enterprise and association have been developed, and Denmark is to day ahead of the largest countries in the export of the products of its soil and of its tenfold increased activity. What lessons are given to the world by this small country!

Are Switzerland, Belgium and Holland less prosperous than their neighbours, because not militarized? Look at the extraordinary expansion of the Scandinavian States, so feeble militarily, but so powerful by reason of their intellectual, moral and economical influence on the whole world.

Can one say that Russia owes its remarkable vitality in all spheres of human activity by reason of the increase of naval and military expenses?

Should we not also mention Canada among others as an example of good and new economical organisation.

The brutal, indisputable fact is this : A powerful military state is to day beaten on the markets of the world by feeble ones incapable of protecting their commerce and colonies otherwise than by their faith in Law and Justice.

Military Supplies must not injure other National Industries.

It is evident that a well governed country must see to have the best rifles, the best guns procurable, if only to protect, in the occurrence and in the present state of the world, its other industries against invasion by surprise. This may be called insurance; we have never contested this, but we consider that the premium of an insurance must be proportional to the means of the owner. To protect industries they must not be sacrificed, and that is what happens when a State, in order to obtain the necessary war material, suspends the production of the essential manufactures of normal life, deprives itself of waggo ˉ locomotives, or orders them from abroad. Such things are en daily, and when we happen to protest, as I have done in Pa. ament on each occasion, I can not own that I am « bleating » . ɪr peace, as it has been said. I simply refuse to howl with the wolves, and I maintain it is more courageous, more patriotic to rise against misuse than to be a party to it. It would be useful to draw up a table and to show side by side the expenses devoted to military supplies and those needed by the national activity of each country and its colonies. All our colleagues have noticed the insufficiency of the budget for public works, agriculture, commerce, education and the incalculable prejudice which this lack of means causes to the essential interests of their country. We see every day that credits are refused for scientific research, when such expense would certainly be productive and would bring forth wealth which the army and navy would share with other public services. But the great inferiority of commerce, agriculture, education, science, is that they interest everyone, that is the working masses, organized or unorganized, whereas military supplies mostly interest a well organized group.

What good would not the great civilising nations have done to the world, had they started by what they must necessarily come to, sooner or later: had they employed in durable works the thousands of millions squandered, the millions of years of work wasted. It is not alone the money which has been spent, it is the normal labour of all the youth of a country diverted from its path every year, it is labour made scarce by the State itself, to the

detriment of agriculture and commerce, of all the industries of
a country.

Who will sum up what this Labour and this Wealth would have
produced if applied to the development of the ressources in which
the world abounds not only in America, Africa, Asia and Australia, but in Europe itself? Who can deny that the worse difficulties of what has been so long called the Oriental Question would
have been avoided or at least attenuated, had the rival powers
agreed to give the Balkan Peninsula and Turkey the first elements of civilisation, railways, roads and schools, instead of
exhausting themselves in armaments. What responsibility for
the powers who have so long maintained barbarity at their
doors by their procrastination, when a general agreement would
have been the salvation of all. How glorious it would have been
for Europe to have vivified by its overflow of activity these territories, some of which, forsaken by God and man, are more
barbarous and more dangerous to cross than many wilds in
America.

Think of the number of bridges constructed, of ships set afloat,
of roads, plantations, of works, of enterprise created, of genius
revealed, what science and activity throughout the world !

What profit for each country, for each individual in this
wealth now squandered in vain. What miscarriage of forces,
of goodwill, of ambition ! Protests begin to rise against
this folly, not only among the anonymous masses or among
revolutionists, but among the industrial classes themselves,
who understand at last that the wrong road has been
followed, and that their interests have been sacrificed.
Nobel and Carnegie, to name only these, are chiefs of
industry. Literature, statistics, politics and the Press have
taken up this idea and the attacks made upon us in the
Press have helped us considerably, as they constitute in
our favour a sort of recommandation, an unequalled advertise-
ment, to independent opinion. Speeches have been made in all
languages, either to distort our ideas, thereby bringing them
better before the public, or to discuss them. Articles for and
against are published daily. Impartial and interesting books
have appeared and have met with universal favour. Such is the
book of Mr. Norman Angell, avowedly launched against our
ideas, but in reality against the « Great Illusion », the folly of
armaments. All this spreads with unsuspected rapidity.

A War of Destruction is no longer possible.

As the public mind becomes educated and perceives that war might often have been avoided in the past by the exercise of a little good sense, and that in future it may be averted by agreement or Arbitration, war no langer appears possible, except as a piece of folly or systematic destruction, exactly as the organisation of Justice does not prevent crime, but makes it an exception. Evidently such a piece of collective folly would be still more exceptional, as a complete organisation, a complicated and public premeditation would be necessary. This would be a universal curse, an outrage on all countries, which would bring them almost automatically together in self-defence against the common danger. This coalition would better come about through the modern instinct of preservation and the natural course of things than through all possible treat

Nowadays the destruction of a c ilised people is more an absurdity than a crime; armies or fl ts may be crushed, but a nation cannot be stamped out : il will resuscitate more incoercible than ever, the so-called destruction firing its vitality.

Neither can the commerce of a rival nation be destroyed; the « *Delenda Carthago* » is out of date. A century ago Benjamin Constant said that to-day Carthage would have all the world in its favour. The commerce of a living country cannot be destroyed; it may be impeded, disturbed, but it will start again with renewed vigour after the war. To declare war on a country in the hope of crushing its commercial superiority is to day a childish dream. The continental blockade which failed a century ago cannot be taken up to-day with any chance of success.

The Machiavelli of our century cannot plead the destruction of the enemy's property as the secret, unavowed cause for war, as this destruction is forbidden on land, and is in a fair way to be forbidden on sea. To violate these rules would be an outrage on the security of all and would cause civilisation to rise up against it. It has often been pointed out that the destruction of the enemy's property on sea would not ruin the belligerents, covered by insurance and having at their disposal, to be largely and freely used, the help of neutrals, too numerous and too active to think of slackening their activity. It is practically impossible to-day to threaten the property and commerce of the enemy without striking at the commerce of the whole world.

Hostilities between two states would be sufficiently disturbing for other states as this would suspend orders and transactions with habitual clients. The stoppage of commerce between these two states would bring about the immediate stoppage of all agricultural and other exports necessary to industry, and as a consequence the stoppage of all work on markets not interested in the conflict. Bankruptcies would be declared everywhere at the same time; innumerable entreprises would be ruined at all points of the globe, entire working populations would be reduced to misery, Governments would be struggling with strikes and perhaps with revolution. The hundreds of millions expended on ammunition for a single battle alone will stand out as an accusation in the eyes of the famished classes, pointing out the millions added to the national debt. We abstain from speaking of the economic and social disturbances which war will beget in the country which will have declared it; we also refrain from comments on the revolts which have taken place on board the warships of two naval powers such at Russia and Brazil in recent times. Then, how shall we conceive that one or both of the belligerents will increase the internal difficulties by paralysing commerce, which is as necessary to either of them as to all?

The aggressor of to-day no longer plays the best part : he is the mar-joy, the common enemy.

Old Legends.
The Protection of Colonies and Maritime Commerce.
Transport of Troops. — The Empire of the Sea.

The protection of colonies is, together with that of commerce and several other well worn legends, a delusion which practical common sense has done away with.

It is clear and has been proved by the experience of Spain and Russia, that a State cannot defend its far-away colonies by means of its fleets without exposing itself to inevitable disaster. The Colonial Empire of a State can only be protected by the good organisation of its colonies, by sound native and foreign policy. England owes the loss of the United States to its wars with France, and France lost India and Louisiana by its continual wars from Louis XIV to Napoleon. The fate of colonies is decided far away from them.

The legend which shows battleships to be necessary to prevent the landing of the enemy is no more worthy of consideration. Landing of troops is always a dangerous operation even in a country without defence, even on friendly soil. It is not conceivable on a hostile shore, inhabited and defended by the inhabitants with all the means of modern science at their disposal to discover and observe the enemy, from submarine navigation, and use of mines to wireless telegraphy and aviation. Without awaiting the advent of this progress, History has supplied us with many examples of the disasters awaiting the landing of troops. No landing can be certain without the toleration or connivance of the enemy, as at Quiberon, and yet, who knows? We know the sequel of these landings. Why is the English expedition on the shores of New Orleans on January 8th 1815 and its defeat never mentioned? The English appeared quite safe, all the advantages were on their side, they had put in line their best chiefs, their best troops, their best fleets and yet a handful of determined men, badly armed and without a fleet was sufficient to drive them back and take away all ᴐire to try again. This battle of New Orleans, of which the Ar .icans are justly proud, is worthy of study. Profitable study ı .ght also be made of the successful landings, but these were always effected by such forces, and yet with what difficulty, thanks to the impotence of the enemy, as in the case of Sidi Ferruch and Sfax. The recent example of Tripoli, surrendering itself, cannot be taken into account.

To land an army in a hostile civilised country is impossible. Napoleon experienced this with England. To maintain this army and to victual it, is still more impossible.

All the arguments which may be brought against this are anachronisms, prior to modern progress.

The case of the transport of troops is similar, which might.it is said, suffice to justify the increase of naval expense. Such transport has been judged by competent seamen as most hazardous and practically impossible. How many dozens of liners would an army corps require? These liners unaccustomed to navigate as fleets, would avoid collision only by steaming at least 500 meters apart from each other, which formation would necessitate a single file, more than twelve miles long, for forty liners to be protected. How many battleships would then be required to flank them?

The empire of the sea is another legend which has been made to glitter before our eyes. The sea belongs to all, as the air belongs to aviation. None can hope to monopolise it, to-day less than ever. England was mistress of the Mediterranean after Aboukir, but this did not prevent Bonaparte returning from Egypt and later Napoleon from Elba.

A century before, at the end of the reign of Louis XIV, the French navy was so enfeebled that England could be considered as mistress of the sea. Yet the audacity of a small number of heroes was enough to intercept communications with Portugal and prevent the sending of troops of succour. The Japanesse arrested the Russian fleet at Tsoushima for several reassons, but first of all because they were at home, defending themselves. Reverse the parts and suppose the Japanese fleet venturing on the American or European coasts; who could say that their chances of success would have been equal? I have said over and over again that if the Russians had devoted the money spent on fleets to the construction of railways or the duplicating of the lines towards the Pacific coast, they would have been better armed, though far from their country, to defend their Asiatic possessions against the Japanese. They were brought to defeat by their fleets. It is to their fleets that they owe the defeat of their armies. Their fleets led them — to say the least — to commit the same error with Japan, as Napoleon with Russia in 1812. Both adventures ended logically and tragically.

On a smaller scale we may mention another example no less conclusive. The barques and fire-ships of Canaris defending the independence of Greece in 1821 had been fatal to many Turkish ships before the crushing blow of Navarino. Such examples could be indefinitely multiplied. Any fleet may disturb or stop commercial navigation in the same way as a few privateers, admitting that our present commerce allowed it. An admiral of genius may dare anything, even to the bombardment of Copenhagen, but no fleet can nowadays be strong enough to guarantee the passage of an army and its arrival at destination.

The oversea transport of troops and their landing must be shelved, together with the idle fancy of protecting commerce and colonies.

Heavy Tonnage.

We cannot disregard the discreet objections of naval men of all countries against heavy tonnage. Opinion is divided on this question, it is true; but it is therefore all the more necessary to bring about the discussion rather than to shirk it; it is our duty. We have no intention to bind any of our colleagues to the opinions expressed in our report. We leave them in perfect independence of judgment, but ask them not to vote blindly. The general objection is that we, parliamentarians, civilians, are incompetent to discuss things pertaining to the army or navy. We are condescendingly informed of them, despite our inability to understand them, and so that we may vote the budgets demanded of us, but we should not in our turn speak of these things. We are asked to vote and keep quiet. It is really absurd to witness this so-called disqualification of parliamentarians and

civilians, when in England, France and the United States the
Secretaries for the Navy are all civilians, who, without any better
preparation than we have, are nevertheless declared competent,
as soon as they approve the expense which we intend to discuss.

I will therefore notwithstanding my incompetence once more
protest against heavy tonnage. Taking the English and Germans
for example, it is evident that the heavy ships are not adapted
to navigation in the North Sea. It is easy to work up opinion
saying that the guns of th heavy battleships will never carry far
enough. This is childi⸌ ⸍he curvature of the earth is here forgotten or left aside ⸌et us not forget that a large battleship
will always be more visible in hazy seas than a small one and
will lose its superiority or armament against an enemy who
can see without being seen. What then is the use of guns carrying
8,000 meters, if the butt is only visible at 400 meters? We have
said, and we repeat it, that a large battleship becomes in these
conditions a mere target and a blind one. But this does not prevent it from costing in construction and armament three
millions of pounds without mentioning the rest.

Inevitable wars.
War between Japan and the United States.

Another legend is that the European States are obliged to increase their armaments, both military and naval, in view of the
inevitable war which must break out and become universal, divi-
ding the world into two armed hosts of which the feeblest must
necessarily disappear. (These are the prognostics of so-called
competent judges.)

This inevitable war should break out between the United
States and Japan. As to this we have made a very complete personal investigation. The results are that both parties not only
desire, but also endeavour and wish to avoid this inevitable
war (1).

If all the arguments which are so freely made use of in favour
of the increase of armaments were carefully weighed, not one
would remain as worthy of attention; on the contrary, one might
ask by what strange prejudice the press of all nations has erected

---

(1) Vide our article of the Temps of July 6th 1911, which was reproduced by the
American Review, The Independent of New York, in June 1911, and by the Japanese paper
Yomi-Uri in July 1911

these false arguments to an imperious doctrine leaving aside
all that could prove its vanity.

We discover every day that History is full of these so-called
inevitable wars which might have been averted. I only call
to mind the wars between France and Russia, useless and
irretrievable slaughters decorated to-day with the name of political errors, formidable and useless wars. I then put on record
the very impartial opinion of one of the men most listened to
in the United States, Dr Benjamin Ide Wheeler, President of the
University of California, expressed to his pupils — a thousand
students of from 18 to 22 years of age. It was to the effect
that the United States had been engaged up till now in three
foreign wars only, with England, Mexico and Spain, and that
all of these could without doubt have been avoided. This means
that the men and money which they cost were sacrificed *for
nothing*. Such words, uttered by such a man, before such an
audience, claim our attention when the pretext for the increase
of armaments is the prospect of the so-called inevitable wars
which in reality none of us desire.

The Organization of Peace is no longer a Dream.

Governments have already felt the necessity and foreseen the
possibility of grouping themselves to adopt a general organization which would answer to the needs of all. The admirable organization of the Universal Postal Union is a daily lesson for the
peoples it has brought together, and since its realisation
innumerable congresses have been held in the interests of the
Commonwealth of Nations. The two Hague Conferences were
represented as unavoidable failures. Nevertheless the first was
followed by the settlement of the unhappy Dogger Bank inci-
dent, and the second by the arbitration of the Casablanca affair
and the settlement of the North American fisheries, to mention
only these three judicial decisions, which restored harmony
between five great military powers : Russia and Great Britain,
Germany, France and the United States.

Clearly defined indications, — besides the two resolutions
before mentioned in favour of the limitation of armaments —
showed the tendencies of the two Hague Conferences and to
what aspirations they aimed and responded.

For example : in 1899 the representatives of the Powers agreed
that, in case of a conflict between two or more States, the other
Powers could no longer remain stolid witnesses, but should, by

right, in duty bound, interve: Art. 27 of the 1899 Convention.)
This word « duty », new   ⌐ncial language, discloses a complete
change of spirit and things; it responds to a new want, recognised by all, the necessity of assuring peace. This, it is true, is
but a moral engagement, but also a written engagement, pro-
ving that Governments recognise that it is necessary and possible for each of them to co-operate for the maintenance of peace.
What more explicit encouragement could Governments give
to public' aspirations? This is an official protest, an attempt at
organized intervention in the common interest.

The Conference of 1907 gave still more force to this 27th Article, which has become Art. 48, by authorising one of the States
in conflict to appeal for intervention and in a way to morally
force its opponent to accept arbitration under penalty of
putting itself in the wrong and stirring public opinion against
its refusal to respond to the appeal. It may be objected that the
country in question might make light of public opinion, but the
important problem is whether bad faith is the last word of
progress, and whether the world is bent on moving forwards or
backwards.

The Interdependence of States.

Taking an unbiassed view of the situation we see that each
country by its exorbitant expense in armaments sacrifices its
interests, compromises its vitality, even its dignity, since it follows in the track of its neighbours without knowing to what
influences the latter obey. This abdication suppresses all serious
parliamentary discussion since the determination of one becomes
law for all. In view of the impossibility for each country to solve
the question of armaments, it evidently becomes an international problem, which should be studied in the common interest of
all. The study of the question as a national problem may greatly
be helped by a general discussion, and it may be the means of
getting out of a dilemma.

The Duty of the Interparliamentary Union.

It behoves the Union to hasten and to prepare these international discussions, since we all tend towards the same goal;
there is no longer any reason to hold back these discussions; on

the contrary, they should be brought forward now that public opinion is educated and understands that it is not intended to encroach on the sovereign right of a State to assure its national defence to the best of its interests. Everyone understands that it is intended to protect the sovereign right of each State against an attempt on its authority, its action, its future. Let us call to mind, to the honour of the Union, that it did not fear to include the question in the programme of the Conference of 1906, and that ever since it has not ceased to keep it in view and to study it.

It is Impossible to draw up a general Plan of Limitation.

It is evident that each country is sole judge of its means of defence which vary from day to day and from one country to another according to its geographical position, its resources, its inventions, its weak points. It is evident, for instance, that stock will have to be taken of the progress as to submarine navigation, quicker with one nation than with another; it is evident also that we must take into account the prodigious success of aerial navigation — the dream of yesterday. which has become the reality of to-day —; this progress may give greater advantage to some than to others, and consequently modify the real proportion of the forces in presence and not only the apparent ones. That is the reason why we have always insisted, as in our report of 1906, on the necessity of a preliminary national study of the question in each country in order to come to a general result. In a word there would be as many schemes as there are nations. Each country must elaborate its own particular scheme in order that from the study of all of these a conclusion based on general interest may be drawn.

These national Studies are urgently required.

At present these national studies may appear as empty dreams but they will rapidly impose themselves in each country under the pressure of urgent necessity, as peaceful solutions regularly take the place of violence, and war becomes more and more rare and impossible. An emulation will be created between States in their efforts to solve the question. This emulation will be more natural than that followed at present for the increase of armaments. When the study of limitation comes to be inscribed on the program of each nation, instead of being put aside with insoluble problems, it will have in its favour all that is now against it. Two or more powers might agree to set an example which others might be induced to follow. Public opinion would be thankful to Governments who would have the courage to seek a reasonable way out of the difficulties in which they are involved. The day is perhaps not far distant when Governments will not dare expose themselves to the reprobation and isolation which their resistance to a wish voiced by all and the common inheritance of progress would shower upon them.

Inevitable Objections.

There is no reason to despair as to the solution of the problem of limitation of armaments. The only objection against it is its novelty. Ten years ago the possibility of an International Arbitration Court was laughed at; yet the Court has been instituted and has given conclusive and decisive results, because the question was ever kept to the fore, and because arbitration has ceased to be a dream and is now a practical and tangible patriotic care. This will be the case with the problem of limitation, when, in the near future, it will be studied as it should be, and not conceived as unpatriotic and impossible to solve.

Then we shall see, and without surprise, our opponents of to-day make use of the arguments which we have vainly put forward during the last ten years, and in the same way as the opponents of arbitration have become its warmest partisans, so shall we see the problem of limitation borne triumphant by those who fought it with the greatest ardour.

Our conscience desires no greater satisfaction.

CONCLUSION.

If, Gentlemen, your share the views which are here set forth, dictated by patriotism and reason, your Commission invites the Interparliamentary Union to energetically maintain its wish of 1906, and to demand that it be taken into consideration by Governments.

It furthermore proposes the following resolution to the next Conference.

RESOLUTION.

The XVIIth Interparliamentary Conference renews the wish expressed and adopted by the London Conference in 1906, as follows :

« The Interparliamentary Conference, considering that the increase of military and naval expenditure which weighs upon the world is universally held to be intolerable, expresses the formal wish that the question of the limitation of armaments be included in the program of the next Conference at the Hague.

» The Conference decides that each group belonging to the Interparliamentary Union shall without delay place this reso-lution before the Government of its Country and exercise its most pressing action on the Parliament to which it belongs, in order that the question of the limitation be the subject of a national study necessary to the ultimate success of the inter-national discussion. »

The XVIIth Interparliamentary Conference records that the problem of the limitation of armaments has not ceased to be, during the last five years, the object of anxiety on the part of both Governments and nations;

That the competition of armaments bids fair to bring about the most serious economical crises which might have the worst consequences for social peace ;

And that in consequence it is urgent, and it is the duty of Governments to seize the first opportunity to discuss the conditions which might bring such competition to an end.

The Interparliamentary Conference invites the different groups to miss no opportunity, notably during the discussion of the Budget, to bring up this question and to invite Governments to undertake, without loss of time, the necessary study to attain, either separately or by means of international agreements, to the realisation of the wish expressed on two different occasions by their Conferences at the Hague.

D'ESTOU ELLES DE CONSTANT,
Member . the Senate (France).
Chairman and Reporter of the Commission.

CONRAD HAUSSMANN,
Member of the Reichstag.
(Germany.)

PAUL MILIOUKOV,
Member of the Duma.
(Russia.)

WEARDALE,
Member of the House of Lords.
(Great Britain.)

Members of the Commission.

CHR.-L. LANGE,
General Secretary of the Interparliamentary Union.

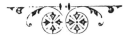

Interparliamentary Union.

17th Conference.

———

LIMITATION OF NAVAL AND MILITARY EXPENDITURE.

———

Text of the resolution adopted by the Council of the Union, at its sitting of April 8th 1911, with the considerations which accompanied it.

At its meeting of the 5th of January 1911, held in Paris, the Commission for the Limitation of naval and military Expenditure agreed to adopt the following Resolution and the considerations which precede it :

The Commission, considering :

1° That during the Interparliamentary Conference in London on the 25th of July 1906 the important discussion of the problem of the Limitation of naval and military expenditure was brought to an end by the unanimous vote of the following resolution :

« The Interparliamentary Conference, considering that the increase of naval and military expenditure which weighs upon the world is universally recognised as intolerable, expresses the wish that the question of limitation be inscribed on the program of the next Hague Conference.

» The Conference decides that each group of the Interparliamentary Union shall, without delay, place this resolution before the Government of its country and exercise its most pressing action on the Parliament to which it belongs, in order that the question of limitation be the object of a national study necessary to the ultimate success of the international discussion »;

2° That this wish has practically received no attention from Governments despite the entreaties and protests of several members of the different groups of the Union;

3° That, notwithstanding, the second Conference at the Hague was not able to abstain in 1907 from uttering a similar opinion and to confirm that expressed by the Conference of 1899, of which the text is given below :

Wish of 1899 :

On the proposal of M. Léon Bourgeois :

« The Conference esteems that the progressive limitation of the armaments which actually weigh upon the world is highly desirable for the moral and material good of Humanity. »

Wish of 1907 :

The Conference unanimously adopted the following resolution :

« The second Peace Conference confirms the resolution adopted by the 1899 Conference in regard to the limitation of military expenditure, and considering that this expenditure has increased since the said year, the Conference declares that it would be highly desirable to see Governments resume the serious study of this question » ;

4° That the different wishes, far from being superficial or subversive, reproduce, in a greatly attenuated manner, the official proposition of the Russian Government as expressed in Count Mouravieff's circular of August 24th 1898, the text of which is reproduced above. These propositions were afterwards taken up by the Governments of Great Britain and the United States on the occasion of the second International Peace Conference;

5° That the possibility of realising these wishes has long been proved in the most happy and conclusive manner by several great military States, by Great Britain and the United States for the whole of the Canadian frontiers, by the United States and Mexico, by the Argentine Republic and Chili;

6° That the considerations expressed in 1898 by the Russian Government in favour of limitation are far from having lost their value; that on the contrary the bid for increase of armaments has not ceased, to the detriment of the divers powers interested, and that several Powers, up till now more or less free

.om this folly, f. i. America, have been touched by the conta-
gious example of this increase;

7° That, despite the difficulty of drawing up reliable general
statistics, it has been possible to show that the total annual
naval and military Expenditure for Europe alone (leaving out
Japan, China and the South American Republics) reached
4,000 millions of francs in 1883, and 7,500 millions in 1908, or
nearly twice as much, totalling close upon 15,000 millions of
francs in 25 years;

That this ruinous increase of expenditure has nevertheless
produced no change in the proportion of the forces of the different powers and has simply brought an added burden to each,
and that progress of modern science often renders useless important work before its completion;

8° That the bid for armaments is in contradiction with the
necessities of competition; that such squandering applied to
unproductive expenditure exasperates all working classes
without distinction, each country having need of its resources
to create and develop its education, hygiene, its machinery and
to work its natural wealth, as also to raise the salaries of the
civil servants in proportion to the increased rate of living;

That from this contradiction, between the adjournment of
useful expenses for peace and the increased and barren expenses
for war, economic crises result more threatening to the world's
peace than the so-called dangers which armaments are intended
to avoid;

9° That general impatience becomes more and more marked
from the fact that all offensive war, even victorious, cannot to-
day be regarded as a solution, inasmuch that it brings with it
hatred and retaliation and must ever be renewed;

That such a waste of activity, wealth and human life, in pure
loss, and to the prejudice of all, clashes with the spirit of our
age;

10° That the progress of the organisation of international justice is sufficiently great and has recently given sufficiently positive results for its non-recognition to appear inexplicable and
derisive;

11° That sound patriotism in each country, coupled with elementary good sense, cannot allow that the research of a suitable
remedy required by the present situation be any longer deferred;

12° That far from weakening the national defence, from which no free man may disinterest himself, a rational and voluntary limitation could but materially and morally strengthen those states which would enter into these views, by allowing them to make a more profitable use of their resources in men and money, and assuring them of the more and more necessary support of the sympathies of public opinion;

13° That recent demonstrations go to show that the economic prosperity of a country is more in an inverse than in a direct ratio of its warlike or military pretentions, and that small States without armies enjoy a real economic privilege in comparison with larger ones;

14° That by a just conception of its own interests the industry of all countries would find in the supplies for the immense works required by peace greater advantages than those it derives from the preparation of war; all countries being at present prevented from making the most indispensable metropolitan and colonial expenditure for their development, such as public works, ports, canals, transports, tunnels, sanitation, reafforestation, fleets of commerce, schools, museums, hospitals, etc., etc.

15° That all terrestrial or maritime war can be avoided by agreement or arbitration, except it be a systematic war of destruction, to-day unavowable and illusory.

16° That, on the other hand, even the destruction of the enemy's property cannot be given as the secret motive for war, since international law, which already insures the respect of the enemy's property on land, is in a fair way to extend the same immunity to property on sea; that, besides, property on sea enjoys to-day and in a certain measure the benefits of maritime insurance without mentioning the ever-increasing facility which allows hostile commerce to make use of the help of neutrals; so that the old threat of destroying the property and commerce of the enemy bears more or less on the commerce of the whole world;

17° That apart from this incontested progress, which tends not only to prevent destructive wars, but leaves them without object, the evident interest of the chief civilised states is to group themselves together without further loss of time to prevent the return of a system of violence and aggression which is no longer in keeping with the development and new exigencies of civilisation; that this necessity for taking general precautions and even for adopting a general scheme of organization in the interest of the collectivity of States has already shown itself by a number of international precautions and measures from the Universal Postal Union to the acts of the two Hague Conferences; that the second Hague Conference notably, by adopting Art. 48 of the Convention for the peaceful settlement of international conflicts completed Art. 27 of the 1899 Convention, and expressly provided that from hence the Powers would not only have the right, but should in duty be bound to offer conciliatory interventions;

18° That in the present state of things the armaments of the different powers are not determined by their own free will, but that each is bound to follow the other at the price of an undisguised abdication of parliamentary power; the result is an evident interdependence of each state towards the other, which has caused the national question of armaments to become an international problem;

19° That it behoves the Union to hasten and to prepare these discussions without of course encroaching upon the sovereign right of each country of assuring its national defence to the best of its interests;

20° That, furthermore, the organization of the national defence and in consequence the estimates of naval and military expenditure varying with each country according to its geographical position, its resources, its weak points, it would be useless and not without great difficulties to seek at present to establish a general scheme, whereas it is natural for each country to study its own particular and national scheme for limitation, or in other words to have as many schemes as there are states;

21° That, when several Governments, respectful of their engagements at the Hague, will decide to openly study this question in a national spirit, each according to its concerns, declaring themselves ready to agree with one or more other states to conclude, in default of a general agreement, special agreements concerning limitation, the study of the question will of itself take rank on the list of all nations among the questions to be solved, instead of being shelved together with impossible problems, and that it will have in its favour all that is accumulated against it to-day;

22° That ten years ago the same objections, the same jeers and the same mistrust were showered on the proposal to institute a Court of Arbitration and that all these objections have been put aside in practice by the settlement of the Hull affair and the arbitration of Casablanca;

23° That it appears in reality to-day in the eyes of public opinion that the study of limitation has not advanced one step simply because it has not been taken up in any country and has not brought about any agreement, having been looked upon as antipatriotic and without issue.

In consequence :

The Commission invites the Interparliamentary Union to energetically maintain its wish of 1906 and to demand that the Governments take it into consideration.

It furthermore proposes the following resolution to the next Conference :

RESOLUTION.

The XVIIth Interparliamentary Conference renews the wish expressed and adopted by the London Conference in 1906, as follows :

« The Interparliamentary Conference, considering that the increase of military and naval expenditure which weighs upon the world is universally held to be intolerable, expresses the formal wish that the question of the limitation of armaments be included in the program of the next Conference at the Hague.

» The Conference decides that each group belonging to the Interparliamentary Union shall without delay place this resolution before the Government of its Country and exercise its most pressing action on the Parliament to which it belongs, in order that the question of the limitation be the subject of a national study necessary to the ultimate success of the international discussion. »

The XVIIth Interparliamentary Conference records that the problem of the limitation of armaments has not ceased to be, during the last five years, the object of anxiety on the part of both Governments and nations ;

That the competition of armaments bids fair to bring about the most serious economical crises which might have the worst consequences for social peace ;

And that in consequence it is urgent, and it is the duty of Governments to seize the first opportunity to discuss the conditions which might bring such competition to an end.

The Interparliamentary Conference invites the different groups to miss no opportunity, notably during the discussion of the Budget, to bring up this question and to invite Governments to undertake, without loss of time, the necessary study to attain, either separately or by means of international agreements, to the realisation of the wish expressed on two different occasions by their Conferences at the Hague.

TABLE OF CONTENTS

APPENDIX.

N° 42764. — Brussels. — Printed by E. Guyot, rue Pachéco, 12.

DATE DUE

NOV 1 1 '80			

DEMCO 38-297